STRATEGIES FOR SUPERIOR CARDIOVASCULAR SERVICE LINE PERFORMANCE

ECG MANAGEMENT CONSULTANTS, INC.

+HCPro

ECG Management Consultants, Inc., Author
Carrie Vaughan, Editor
Rick Johnson, Executive Editor
Matt Cann, Group Publisher
Doug Ponte, Cover Designer
Janell Lukac, Graphic Artist

Genevieve d'Entremont, Copyeditor
Liza Talbot, Proofreader
Matt Sharpe, Production Supervisor
Susan Darbyshire, Art Director
Jean St. Pierre, Senior Director of Operations

Advice given is general. Readers should consult professional counsel for specific legal, ethical, or clinical questions. Arrangements can be made for quantity discounts. For more information, contact:

HCPro, Inc.
75 Sylvan Street, Suite A-101
Danvers, MA 01923
Telephone: 800/650-6787 or 781/639-1872
Fax: 781/639-2982
E-mail: *customerservice@healthleadersmedia.com*

HCPro, Inc., is the parent company of HealthLeaders Media.

Visit HCPro at its World Wide Web sites:
www.healthleadersmedia.com, www.healthleadersmedia.com/marketing,
www.hcpro.com, and *www.hcmarketplace.com*

Contents

    Strategies for Superior Cardiovascular Service Line Performance

About the Authors

M. Sue Anderson, Senior Manager

Ms. Anderson's area of focus is cardiac services, particularly cardiac service line development, strategic planning, and hospital/physician affiliations. She has designed cardiovascular (CV) service line strategies for more than 12 hospitals and academic medical centers (AMC) in the past two years and has spoken at several national conferences on trends in CV service line management and governance. Ms. Anderson also leads ECG Management Consultants' CV Services Affinity Group, which is responsible for developing thought leadership in CV services. Ms. Anderson holds a Master of Business Administration from the UCLA Anderson School of Management and bachelor's degrees in English and finance from the University of Richmond.

Ross A. Armstrong, Manager

Mr. Armstrong works in ECG's Healthcare practice. His background in both hospital administration and healthcare consulting has provided him with a range of skills that include strategic planning, financial analysis, facility and operational planning, and physician integration planning. He has previously managed operational improvement and large capital asset planning projects. Mr. Armstrong has master's degrees in health services administration and business administration from the University of Alabama at Birmingham.

Christopher T. Collins, Principal

Mr. Collins, a principal in the Boston office of ECG, works with boards and executive leadership of academic health centers on a diverse range of strategic and business planning initiatives including integrated center/institute development and physician/hospital alignment. Specialty areas of focus include cancer, cardiovascular, and neurosciences. He has nearly 15 years of experience in the provider sector and holds a master's degree in health services administration from The George Washington University.

Joshua D. Halverson, Principal

As an ECG consultant, Mr. Halverson has worked with AMCs on projects relating to strategy design, financial analysis, and business planning. He has expertise in evaluating and designing economic arrangements between medical schools and affiliated teaching hospitals. Prior to joining ECG in 2000, Mr. Halverson worked in the healthcare strategy practice of a nationally recognized management consulting firm. He holds master's degrees in healthcare administration and public health from the University of Minnesota Carlson School of Management, with concentrations in financial management and quantitative methods.

Michelle L. Holmes, Senior Manager

Ms. Holmes joined ECG in 2005 with extensive experience in implementing an electronic health record (EHR) in a large, ambulatory healthcare system where she played a key role in the successful adoption of the EHR at the system's cardiology practices. She has served as project adviser/manager and has provided quality assurance oversight for several major practice management and EHR implementations across the country. She has also been involved in implementation strategy and curriculum design, clinician and clinical information system support staff training, decision support and population management tool development, standardized clinical report development and distribution, and system upgrade processes. Ms. Holmes has master's degrees in business administration and health services administration from the University of Washington.

Kevin M. Kennedy, Principal

A consultant since 1990, Mr. Kennedy has assisted dozens of hospitals, health systems, and medical groups with their strategic, financial, and operational challenges. He has expertise in operations improvement, hospital/physician relationships, and physician compensation planning. Recently, he's developed several hospital/physician cardiac joint ventures, facilitated cardiology practice acquisitions, redesigned compensation plans for hospital-employed cardiologists and CV surgeons, and conducted operations improvement studies in both inpatient and outpatient settings. He holds a Master of Business Administration from The University of Chicago and a Bachelor of Science in business administration from The University of Arizona.

Managed Care Services Affinity Group

ECG's Managed Care Services Affinity Group is responsible for the thought leadership and knowledge development of the firm's Managed Care Contracting practice, which focuses on all matters related to provider reimbursement. The group has extensive experience in the area of managed care and provider reimbursement, including strategy development, the development of reimbursement structures, health plan contract negotiations, and operations. Key contributions were made by the following members of the group:

- Ms. Terri L. Welter, principal, leads the firm's managed care contracting practice. She has more than 15 years of experience assisting hospitals and medical groups in the financial planning, assessment, and negotiation of their health plan contracts.

- Mr. Charles A. Brown, senior manager, has extensive experience assisting hospitals and medical groups in the financial planning and turnaround of their managed care contracts. He has held a range of management positions in the managed care industry.

- Mr. James P. Donohue, senior manager, has more than 15 years of experience in the healthcare industry working with large healthcare systems and has conducted dozens of consulting engagements focused on business operations and strategic planning, reimbursement strategies, and contracting.

- Ms. Purvi B. Bhatt, manager, is one of the firm's reimbursement experts and focuses on health plan contract negotiations, contract modeling, and financial performance improvement for hospitals and medical groups.

- Mr. Jason C. Lee, manager, is one of the firm's provider performance experts and focuses on projects related to managed care contracting, reimbursement planning and analysis, hospital/medical group alignment, and physician compensation.

Stephen F. Messinger, Principal

Mr. Messinger has extensive experience in strategic and business planning, business development, mergers and acquisitions, and managed care. He has worked with a broad range of healthcare organizations and has assisted hospitals, health systems, and physician groups in CV strategy development and performance improvement. Mr. Messinger earned a Master of Health Services Administration from The George Washington University and a Bachelor of Science in clinical sciences from Cornell University.

Kathryn K. Reed, Manager

Ms. Reed has broad experience in strategic planning, financial analysis, service line development, and hospital/physician alignment. She has expertise in CV services and has worked with numerous clients on their CV service line and programmatic needs. In addition, she is a member of the firm's cardiovascular affinity group and helped spearhead ECG's recently published *Cardiovascular Service Line Management Survey – Key Findings and Implications*, publication date 2009 based on 2008 data, in partnership with Thomson Reuters.

Ms. Reed holds a master of business administration degree from the University of Washington Michael G. Foster School of Business and a bachelor of science degree in biology from The University of Texas at Austin.

About ECG

 ECG offers a broad range of strategic, financial, operational, and technology-related consulting services to healthcare providers. As a leader in the industry, ECG provides specialized expertise to community hospitals, academic medical centers, health systems, and medical groups. For nearly 40 years, its approximately 80 consultants have played an instrumental role in developing and implementing innovative and customized solutions that effectively address issues confronting healthcare providers. ECG has offices in Seattle, Boston, Washington, D.C., San Diego, and St. Louis.

At the heart of its expertise in CV services is an understanding of the competencies needed to differentiate top-performing CV service lines. ECG has had the pleasure of working with premier CV programs, helping them build and develop service line strategies and structures. In addition, it has conducted industry-leading research to understand the mechanics of the best-in-class programs.

Creating a Successful Cardiovascular Service Line

The market dynamics for cardiovascular (CV) services are changing rapidly, driven by new approaches to payment, more educated consumers, mandatory outcomes reporting, and purchasers searching for greater value. In the past, hospitals focused on creating a positive image or brand identity. Today, the solid reputation of a hospital in the community no longer ensures success. Rather, each of a hospital's clinical programs will succeed or fail based on its individual ability to respond to the needs of three separate constituencies— patients, payers, and physicians. This is especially true of CV programs. There is clear evidence that patients, payers, and physicians are beginning to shop not just for the best hospital, but also for specific programs that can demonstrate their value by combining clinical quality, economic efficiency, and patient satisfaction. Medicare demonstration projects showcasing bundled payments are a harbinger of future reimbursement schemes that will attempt to align incentives across various parts of the healthcare system, and the service line organizational structure seems ideally suited to this new environment. Because of the large dollar amounts involved and the prestige associated with a quality CV program, we believe these issues will affect CV programs sooner and more acutely than other service lines.

In response to these pressures, most hospitals have taken at least preliminary steps to develop CV service line structures that improve performance, encourage physician involvement, and seek to gain competitive advantage. The level of this activity varies widely, from those just initiating the service line to those that have a decade or more of experience and may be on their third or fourth permutation. Even though there are remarkable success stories, most hospitals' CV service line activity is still a work in progress, and in many facilities, the CV service line is stagnant or foundering.

Understanding service line principles and options is essential to ensuring that a hospital's CV program can reach its potential. The first key point to understand is that the decision to organize CV programs as a service line is not monolithic. It should be thought of as at least eight different decisions, each of which can be considered separately. Although these issues are related, CV program design can and should be tailored to your hospital's specific needs and environment.

Introduction to Service Line Principles

A service line is organized around patient diagnosis to provide coordination of care and accessibility of information over time, regardless of where the care is provided or who provides it. Service lines are typically recognizable to patients and caregivers as rational collections of inpatient and ambulatory services that a patient may require during treatment for an episode or condition.

 Strategies for Superior Cardiovascular Service Line Performance

What features characterize a service line?

For years, hospitals have advanced a range of programs under the heading "service line," but a center of excellence, product line marketing, logo, or an occasional team meeting does not constitute a mature service line unless the following features are also present:

- Is recognized by physicians, management, and patients as a collection of services needed for specified conditions

- Provides a single point of patient access throughout the treatment process

- Offers coordinated provider teams for patient-based services and care

- Incorporates standardized processes, protocols, and outcome measurements

- Reports financial, operational, and quality-of-care data at the service line level

- Demands full alignment of physicians, staff, and management across all sites of care

- Offers participation in strategic, operational, and financial decision-making for key providers

- Has a unified management control structure that governs critical operations and the strategy regarding service line delivery assets

What services should be structured as a service line?

Consideration for a service line should focus first on those areas where the hospital has established experience. Progress will be more rapid and greater value will be created by organizing existing expertise rather than starting from scratch. Second, the service must have a significant ambulatory component because coordinating services and clinical information across varying sites is what adds value for stakeholders. Third, the service must have the potential for profitability. If increasing market share only leads to greater financial losses, investing time and money is difficult to justify. Finally, service lines typically have an element of multidisciplinary care that benefits from the coordination and superior information flow that service lines provide.

CV programs are arguably the most common service lines to be developed by a hospital, followed by oncology, women and children, neuroscience, and orthopedics. These services meet the criteria introduced earlier and are often a priority for payers in terms of demonstrating quality and efficiency in the delivery of care. Smaller and/or more narrowly focused programs can also meet the criteria for service line development and should be given consideration—especially if physician leadership is available.

Key Elements for Service Line Success

When considering a new service line or enhancing an existing service line, the following eight key elements must be addressed.

1. Service line composition

The first and most basic question might be, "What services are included?" This question may seem simple at first glance, but determining which activities should be managed by the service line structure gets significantly more complex when you consider that many of these services could be claimed by multiple hospital departments. CV surgery, for example, could be part of the operating room (OR) or part of a CV service line. Similarly, many CV imaging services could "belong" to the diagnostic imaging department. (Figure 1.1 shows a typical list of CV services that most would agree are appropriate for a fully developed service line.) The decision of which services should be controlled by CV service line governance and management features is therefore critical and often fraught with internal "turf battles."

FIGURE 1.1

TYPICAL SERVICES INCLUDED IN A COMPREHENSIVE CV SERVICE LINE

Screening and Early Detection	Treatment, Diagnosis, and Follow-Up	Support Services	Education and Outreach
• Blood pressure. • Carotid Doppler. • Cholesterol testing. • Diabetes screening. • Dietary consultation. • ECG. • Echocardiogram. • Electrophysiology consultation. • Exercise stress test. • Noninvasive imaging. • Screening for peripheral artery disease.	• Angiography. • Calcium scoring. • Cardiac surgery. • Catheterization. • Heart failure management. • Interventional cardiology. • Pacemaker/ICD implant. • Medical therapies. • MRI/PET. • Radiofrequency ablation.	• Cardiac rehabilitation. • Diet and exercise consultation. • Mental health counseling. • Palliative and supportive care. • Smoking cessation.	• Community seminars, CME for physicians. • Dietary consultations. • Pamphlets. • Participation in turnkey programs. • Self-assessment risk questionnaires.

2. Management/organizational models

Service lines are emerging as the organizational backbone of many hospitals, with well-defined business units replacing the traditional "siloed" organizational structure. There is a continuum of organizational ideas on how to best run a service line (see Figure 1.2).

Organizations seeking benefits of the service line concept without radical adjustments to their organizational structure often begin with creating a "coordinator" position. This role typically represents the service line in organizational decisions but has no actual operating authority. The coordinator role is often a thankless one, since this individual has accountability for CV program development and progress but has no formal authority to make the changes required to

FIGURE 1.2

RANGE OF MANAGEMENT STRUCTURES UTILIZED

Model	Description	Relative Effort Required to Implement	Relative Effectiveness
Matrixed	Key and shared service line areas have an indirect reporting relationship to service line coordinator.	Medium	Low to Medium (Depending on Physician Alignment and Senior Leadership Commitment)
Partially Consolidated	Key service line areas are under the direct control of service line administrator. Shared services have an indirect reporting relationship.	Medium to High	Medium to High (Depending on Physician Alignment and Senior Leadership Commitment)
Fully Integrated	All areas within the service line report directly to service line administrator, who is fully dedicated to service line management.	High	Medium to High (Depending on Ability to Integrate with Nursing)

achieve these goals. Instead, this position will succeed or fail based on the ability to influence individuals through persuasion, data, and appeals to the greater good of the institution. Strong executive support is required for this position to be successful—and a well-functioning governance structure is also helpful.

Some of the key decision-making authorities that generally vary with the service line model chosen are budgetary control and hiring and termination of staff and physicians within the service line. Organizations that invest the service line leader with real authority by giving him or her these management responsibilities can dramatically increase the effectiveness of the service line lead, almost irrespective of structure. However, if an organization is seeking the most integrated model and does not provide the leadership with these responsibilities, it will substantially suboptimize the ability of management to achieve the desired results of the more highly integrated model.

The next step is to assign operational accountability to the service line manager. Typically, the direct-reporting areas are those that do not significantly interact with other hospital departments. For CV services, the only easy decision is the cath labs, and even that is challenged by vascular surgeons and interventional radiologists, who see these labs as critical to their own success and may resent the influence provided to cardiologists under a service line. As with any matrix structure, it is critical to specifically define what is signified by the dotted line (see Figure 1.3).

FIGURE 1.3

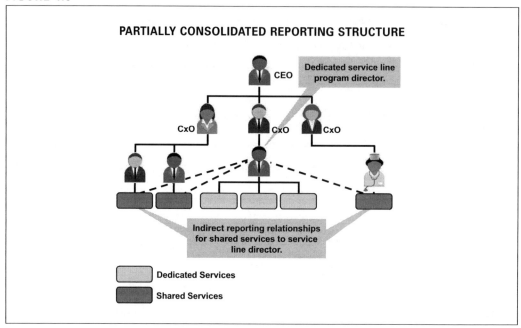

PARTIALLY CONSOLIDATED REPORTING STRUCTURE

Under a fully integrated model, the health system views the service line as the primary organizational unit. Ideally, support services departments (nursing, information technology, finance, etc.) will view the CV service line director as an important client, and he or she will report directly to the chief operating officer or CEO. Like the other structures, this model has trade-offs, specifically that decisions can sometimes be made in a vacuum without fully considering the impact on non-CV departments. However, physicians and managers tend to enjoy this structure the most since it simplifies the decision-making process. This structure typically requires significant scale to be effective.

3. Governance structures

The allocation of resources and close coordination of services across sites of care, physician specialties, ancillary services, and support departments are central to effective CV service line development. Policies, procedures, and protocols need to be developed that are distinct from those of the traditional hospital, and these should be based on collaboration between providers and managers. The governance structure determines, to a large extent, who makes key operating decisions affecting CV services and how those decisions are made.

The complexities of service line management and the difficulties of breaking down barriers between multiple care disciplines demand a high level of physician involvement. A service line governance structure that engages physicians will not only result in massive improvements in decision-making and resource allocation, but also will secure physician commitment to service line success.

When developing a service line governance structure, it is necessary to consider how representation will be determined, specifically the number of seats and how they might be apportioned across groups, specialties, or campuses. (See Figure 1.4 for a full range of CV service line governance structures). This is critical for CV services because of the potential for conflict across specialties.

FIGURE 1.4

RANGE OF CV SERVICE LINE GOVERNANCE STRUCTURES COMMONLY UTILIZED

	Limited Governance	Ad Hoc Committee	Standing Committee	Leadership Board
Overview	▪ No established mechanism for governance. Individuals informally consulted.	▪ Formed to discuss specific issues (e.g., new products, workforce planning) as they arise	▪ Established governance body responsible for wide range of oversight functions	▪ Board maintains complete accountability for service line performance reporting directly to hospital CEO
Strategic Planning	▪ No role	▪ Informed	▪ Advisory	▪ Advice, direction, and approval
Management Selection	▪ No role	▪ Input into hiring	▪ Input into hiring, performance review	▪ Accountability for hiring and firing
Budgeting	▪ No role	▪ Occasional advisory	▪ Advisory	▪ Advice and approval
Physician Composition	▪ Individual physicians may be consulted	▪ Limited physician involvement	▪ Significant physician composition	▪ Majority physician composition

4. Management composition

The question of day-to-day management and accountability for performance of the service line is often given too little thought. A service line administrator can be given responsibility for operations. Although management by an administrator is familiar and easy to implement, the interdisciplinary nature of service lines and the increasing importance of clinical standardization suggest that a physician medical director should be part of the team. Shared management responsibility can be difficult to implement, but it is central to creating both quality and efficiency in a CV service line. Alternative approaches to management are shown in Figure 1.5.

   Strategies for Superior Cardiovascular Service Line Performance

FIGURE 1.5

ALTERNATIVE APPROACHES TO SERVICE LINE LEADERSHIP

Administrative Director	Physician Leader	Dyad Leadership
Philosophy: A highly trained, experienced manager who understands the organizational, operational, and financial implications of running a successful service line is best equipped to lead these complex enterprises.	Philosophy: Physician leaders may be best prepared to ensure quality and safety, achieve patient outcome goals, pursue service development opportunities, and foster relationships with key physicians.	Philosophy: The benefits of having both the clinical expertise of a physician and the business experience of an administrator may outweigh the added complexity that accompanies a dyad leadership structure.
Benefits and Concerns	**Benefits and Concerns**	**Benefits and Concerns**
■ An experienced administrator may have a better understanding of the business aspects related to service line organization and development. ■ It may be easier to facilitate effective communication between administrative staff and physicians. ■ The medical staff may relate better to a physician leader.	■ Physicians have a unique understanding of the healthcare environment, which may result in improved patient outcomes and clinical coordination. ■ It may be easier to recruit top physician talent under this model. ■ It is difficult to find a physician leader who has business experience and can balance the clinical and management demands of the position.	■ Each leader brings a specialized skill set to the organization, integrating a patient care and clinical focus with a hospital business focus. ■ A more effective line of communication is created between administrative and medical staff. ■ A dual reporting relationship introduces additional complexities into the system. ■ Lines of authority may blur, leading to confusion or inefficiencies.

5. Physician alignment

The critical objectives of most CV programs—growth, patient care protocols, outcome measures, enhanced patient experiences, and meaningful efficiency improvements—are not likely to emerge from traditional relationships between hospitals and independent physicians. The basic alternatives to unaffiliated practices are to offer medical directorships (essentially buying clinical input); develop contractual relationships (lease arrangements, joint ventures, gain sharing, etc.); or to employ physicians. There are benefits and drawbacks to each of the options. However, our experience suggests that a combination of approaches may be most useful and practical, depending on the unique characteristics of each situation.

In addition to the relationship between physicians and the hospital, consideration should be given to the relationships among different CV specialties that will be part of the service line. The interdisciplinary nature of CV services places a premium on cooperation between physicians, and so ensuring the desired level of collaboration, especially among physicians who may be competing for patients or resources, is a major management challenge (see Figure 1.6 for some of the structural variety in these relationships and the implications of each).

FIGURE 1.6

PHYSICIAN ALIGNMENT CONSTRUCTS

State of Alignment	Description	Strategic Priorities
Competition A C B D	Each subspecialist is independently affiliated with the hospital. Clinical integration is lacking, and groups compete for patients and available resources.	■ Forming a strong, physician-led governance body. ■ Building trust and coordination between groups through modest joint initiatives (e.g., service line dashboards, joint outreach clinics, coordinated physician referrals).
Coordination A C B D	Subspecialists remain independent but take a coordinated approach to referral relationships and physician recruitment.	■ Clearly aligning economic incentives. ■ Developing more complex joint service line initiatives, such as program development and service line marketing.
Combination A C B D	Some specialists remain independent, while others are formally employed by the hospital.	■ Building trust between employed and independent physicians. ■ Aligning the financial incentives of all physicians regardless of employment status.
Coalition A C B D	All subspecialists are employed, resulting in a unified and coordinated physician workforce. Program planning, resource allocation, and physician recruitment are aligned.	■ Developing a compensation plan that aligns physician and service line incentives and accounts for the unique needs of each individual subspecialty. ■ Ensuring physician engagement in service line planning and governance.

6. Financial management

Hospital financial management systems—characterized by granular "cost centers" and more general revenue reports—are not well suited to the

 Strategies for Superior Cardiovascular Service Line Performance

cross-divisional and multidisciplinary management needs of most service lines. To accurately measure financial performance, each service line should be accounted for as if it were a separate business unit, with all revenue and all costs for each patient allocated back to the service line. For example, if a CV service line patient is seen in the clinic and then has a CV surgical procedure and a three-day hospital stay, the revenue from all three services should be credited to the service line. Likewise, the cost associated with each service should be charged to the service line through a system of transfer pricing within the hospital. (See Figure 1.7 for the range in financial reporting structures.) This may be difficult to achieve, but basing accounting on service lines can provide significantly improved data for the management of the organization, enabling better decisions on resource allocation.

FIGURE 1.7

RANGE OF FINANCIAL REPORTING STRUCTURES

Model	Description	Considerations	Relative Effort and Effectiveness
Traditional Reporting	Traditional structure; each cost department is accountable for creating and maintaining its own budget (e.g., cath lab, OR, and cardiology clinic all have separate budgets and financial statements).	▪ Requires no additional implementation. ▪ Necessitates a manual collection process. ▪ Provides ambiguous reports on overall service line performance because of different reporting systems.	Low
Structured Service Line Reporting	Partially integrated financial structure; some financial reporting methods are consolidated to provide more comprehensive service line performance reports.	▪ Requires the development of a standardized reporting process to ensure the development of comparable financial reports. ▪ Provides some indication of overall performance, but results are often still ambiguous. ▪ Is a somewhat labor-intensive process.	Medium (Depending on Extent of Decision Support Services)
Integrated Service Line Reporting	Fully integrated financial structure; the cardiac service line has one budget for all cardiac-related facility and management services and reports integrated financial statements.	▪ Offers the most accurate method for assessing service line performance. ▪ Requires a more comprehensive financial reporting system. ▪ May be a labor- and cost-intensive implementation process.	High (Depending on Extent of Decision Support Services)

7. Facilities

From a patient's perspective, nothing says "organized care" more clearly than being able to see all major components of the continuum of care immediately upon entering the lobby. Proximity of related services is inherently comforting to patients. From a practical standpoint, locating related services near each other provides opportunities for information sharing, reduced travel time for staff, and more immediate identification of work flow and bottleneck issues.

Dedicated "heart hospitals" are the ultimate ambition of nearly all CV service line managers, and are among the most difficult to achieve due to constraints on capital, real estate, and the necessity of shared services that support other hospital departments. Nevertheless, a facility strategy needs to be part of any service line plan. This is inherently more difficult for CV services that tend to blend inpatient and outpatient services. At a minimum, a hospital should group service line components as close together as is practical. Other details, such as a dedicated entry and common signage, will provide comfort to patients, impart a sense of coordination, and help establish a brand identity. Since most CV patients will visit a physician before needing a hospital stay, integrating CV clinics with hospital-based services should be a priority. (See Figure 1.8 for the continuum of facility options.)

        Strategies for Superior Cardiovascular Service Line Performance

FIGURE 1.8

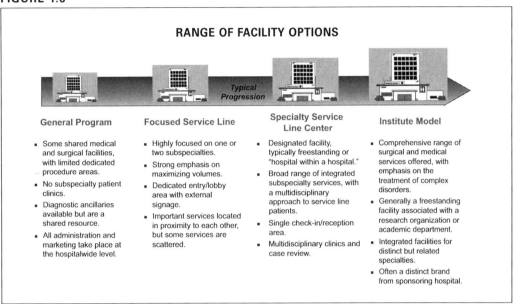

RANGE OF FACILITY OPTIONS

Typical Progression

General Program	Focused Service Line	Specialty Service Line Center	Institute Model
▪ Some shared medical and surgical facilities, with limited dedicated procedure areas. ▪ No subspecialty patient clinics. ▪ Diagnostic ancillaries available but are a shared resource. ▪ All administration and marketing take place at the hospitalwide level.	▪ Highly focused on one or two subspecialties. ▪ Strong emphasis on maximizing volumes. ▪ Dedicated entry/lobby area with external signage. ▪ Important services located in proximity to each other, but some services are scattered.	▪ Designated facility, typically freestanding or "hospital within a hospital." ▪ Broad range of integrated subspecialty services, with a multidisciplinary approach to service line patients. ▪ Single check-in/reception area. ▪ Multidisciplinary clinics and case review.	▪ Comprehensive range of surgical and medical services offered, with emphasis on the treatment of complex disorders. ▪ Generally a freestanding facility associated with a research organization or academic department. ▪ Integrated facilities for distinct but related specialties. ▪ Often a distinct brand from sponsoring hospital.

8. Information management

For a CV service line to be successful, it should be able to demonstrate that its outcomes are better, its costs of care are lower, and its patient satisfaction is high—in short, that it is providing greater value than its competitors. The driving principle of service lines is that coordination of services creates improved quality and efficiency. Gathering and reporting data that measures performance is crucial and is a major shortcoming in many of the service line initiatives that we have reviewed. Database requirements for a fully developed service line include:

- Patient encounters by site

- Diagnosis

- Treatments

- Outcomes of care

- Cost of care by diagnosis and treatment

- Financial performance of the service line

- Patient satisfaction

Furthermore, each of the metrics needs both internal and external benchmarks to measure improvement and to demonstrate performance relative to competitors. CV surgery is among the most measured and benchmarked services provided anywhere in the hospital, and most top programs invested long ago in the necessary staffing and information resources to measure performance and outcomes. Committed CV programs devote the financial and staffing resources to utilize these databases and track institutional progress against these measures.

Implementation Issues

The theoretical considerations of the service line design elements discussed in this chapter can present challenges, but in practice these may seem trivial compared to the implementation barriers. We have found two major potential roadblocks to service line implementation: institutional culture and physician leadership.

Institutional culture

Service lines demand the integration of traditionally siloed hospital functions. While this is a positive development, it represents potentially significant change within the established hospital hierarchy. Management in nursing, finance, ancillary services, and employed physician clinics will be challenged to respond to service lines' needs in these environments. For instance, nursing within a service line may entail staffing for physician offices, diagnostic and procedure centers, patient education programs, and inpatient care. CV service line leadership will seek nurses with specific expertise who are dedicated to that service line and accountable to service line management. This may mean different pay levels for nurses, resistance to "floating" service line nurses to another unit, and a claim of ownership of the nursing staff by the service line. Nursing administration may have legitimate concerns related to education and enforcement of nursing standards and may resist accommodating such changes.

Other hospital departments and members of the medical staff will face similar pressures, and intramural disputes can be expected. For hospital executives, the technical challenge of how best to organize a CV service line may end up seeming easy compared with the management challenge of getting employees to embrace it.

Physician leadership

CV service line development demands tight alignment of physician and hospital interests, and getting there is often the most challenging aspect of service line management. Regardless of the structures used to align with physicians, hospitals with successful service lines acknowledge the requirement of physician champions and the importance of ceding true clinical and operational power to physician leaders.

Physicians, for their part, often do not realize that the input they have long sought can be achieved through service line management. Few hospitals have ongoing programs to identify and develop physician leaders, and many of our clients find it frustrating to cultivate signature programs because physician leadership cannot be found. From a different perspective, many of our academic health system clients have built distinguished clinical service lines due in large part to the power and vision of clinical department chairs.

Unfortunately, it is rare for a community hospital to have a physician with both the interest and the ability to lead a service line. So it is tempting to appoint the physician with the strongest technical skills to this position, the assumption being that the physician's strong clinical reputation corresponds with his or her ability to lead. However, the skills required for this type of role more often resemble those of a compromise-crafting politician. Often, the hospital has to identify a doctor with potential and then work to create the interest and skills necessary to be an effective leader. Hiring from the outside should be carefully thought out, since there is a danger of antagonizing existing providers. The challenge for CEOs is to first acknowledge the importance of physician leadership and then invest in the structure needed to make it happen.

The Future for CV Service Lines

It is appropriate to ask if service lines are simply the most recent manifestation of a 30-year organizational fad or if they will have a long-term impact on hospitals. Existing trends point toward the likely future direction of service lines. In the near term, hospitals will probably be focusing on the one, two, or three service lines that can best attract patients, providers, and payer contracts. For many hospitals, if not most, this will include the CV program. In this short-term scenario, service lines are essentially an "add-on" to the organization's business. Over time, however, service lines have the potential to *be* the organization's central business. Today's generalist hospital with limited coordination between hospital and ambulatory services will be replaced by coordinated groupings of inpatient and outpatient facilities interconnected by a shared organizational culture, value-driven leadership, and IT infrastructure. In most of today's tertiary centers and advanced community hospitals, an advanced CV service line will be a critical component of that structure.

The underlying (perhaps unsettling) implication is that many hospitals and health systems are not likely to remain as full-service providers. Providing the full range of services to all patients is simply not going to work in an era of focused competition, limited resources, and empowered patients. With the increased availability of effectiveness data to both payers and patients, services must be highly rated for both cost and quality or they will fail in a competitive marketplace. Thus, it is likely that markets will be split up by service line, with a relatively small number of providers in each niche and "turf battles" in emerging or contested services. We are starting to see the beginning of this evolution, with payer requests for proposals for services that are costly yet data-rich—especially CV services.

Fundamentally, service line development must be viewed as a major organizational commitment, and service lines should be carefully nurtured over time. It is likely that the future of an organization's service lines will determine the future of the organization as a whole. Since many organizations have begun this transformational process with their CV programs, it may well be this critical service that sets the tone for the future of the organization and plays a critical role in its ability to compete in a very different healthcare landscape.

Strategies for Superior Cardiovascular Service Line Performance

Service Line Strategic Planning

"Vision without action is a daydream; action without vision is a nightmare."

This Japanese proverb outlines a key tenet of strategic planning. For a strategic plan to be successful, it must be driven by a clear and compelling vision. At the same time, an effective strategic planning process must result in practical and actionable strategies. It must provide the overall direction needed to focus the organization's efforts and resources, as well as produce the strategies to ensure that the identified direction can be achieved. A successful strategic plan is built upon the following three distinct characteristics:

- **Focus** – What the hospital does and does not do in pursuit of its objectives to provide market-leading services to patients and physicians

- **Differentiation** – How the hospital creates value for patients and physicians in a way that is different from its competitors

- **Fit** – The unique combination of activities that leverages the hospital's strengths and locks out competitors

Ultimately, strategic planning is a resource prioritization and allocation process. The hospital should decide where there is the most potential and where it should focus its financial and human resources. By creating a CV service line, hospital leadership has taken the first step in making cardiac services a focal point of the hospital. Within the service line, however, it is still necessary to decide what initiatives should be funded. The strategic planning process should result in an improvement in both the organization's competitive position and its financial situation. Execution of the strategic plan should be outcome-oriented, guided by focused measures of success. A key role of the strategic planning process is the development of consensus among the organization's stakeholders regarding how future success will be measured, monitored, and achieved.

Physicians are a critical strategic resource, and sound hospital/physician relationships are key to success. This is particularly important in CV service line planning, as physicians must be an integral component of the vision for the service line and must also support the strategic direction. As such, the strategic planning process should be inclusive of a broad base of key physician leaders, including all specialties and employed and private practice physicians. They should be treated as partners of the hospital, and their perspectives should be considered in the strategic planning process. To ensure successful implementation, it is critical for physicians to own the strategic plan.

A fundamental aspect of cardiac service line strategic planning is a clear progression from vision to goals to strategies to tactics. The vision and goals guide how the cardiac program ultimately serves its patients, physicians, staff, and community. Developing a program vision up front is an essential part of establishing a cardiac program that has a sustainable advantage—a program that is focused, differentiated, and competitive. From the vision and goals come the strategies that form the framework of the initiatives to support the vision. The tactics describe in more granular terms how the strategies will be achieved and pave the way for implementation planning. This strategic planning framework is depicted in Figure 2.1.

FIGURE 2.1

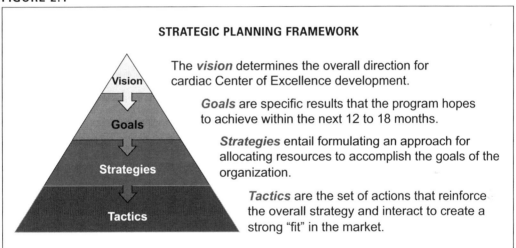

STRATEGIC PLANNING FRAMEWORK

Vision

Goals

Strategies

Tactics

The *vision* determines the overall direction for cardiac Center of Excellence development.

Goals are specific results that the program hopes to achieve within the next 12 to 18 months.

Strategies entail formulating an approach for allocating resources to accomplish the goals of the organization.

Tactics are the set of actions that reinforce the overall strategy and interact to create a strong "fit" in the market.

Key Elements of Strategic Planning

Involve all key stakeholders

A successful CV strategic plan cannot be developed in isolation, but should include all key stakeholders to ensure the optimal chances for success. If a strategic plan is developed that does not consider the perspectives of physicians, it will be very difficult to gain the buy-in and support needed to drive implementation. The same can be said of all the stakeholder groups, including finance, marketing, planning, and nursing. The value of being inclusive should be balanced with a process that is not hindered by an overly large steering committee and an inefficient decision-making process. It is important to develop a clear work plan at the outset, carefully choose a representative steering committee, and involve other stakeholders as needed via interviews and/or select meetings, which would provide input at key junctures.

The steering committee guiding the CV strategic planning process should include both hospital leadership as well as physicians. It is our experience that a steering committee of approximately 12 or less members is most efficient in terms of size; however, more important than determining the number of members is selecting the right individuals to participate. Steering committee members from the hospital typically include the service line administrator, director of the employed physician practice (if applicable), COO or CEO, representatives from finance and planning, and a nursing leader. To ensure inclusive representation from the medical staff, physicians from each specialty within the service line should be asked to attend. These are often the medical directors of cardiology, cardiac surgery, vascular surgery, and interventional radiology (if considered part of the service line). If some physicians within the service line are employed, balance must be achieved by including employed and private practice physicians to ensure that both feel that they are an important part of the process.

When considering which physicians to include on the steering committee, part of the decision should be based on who is seen as a thought leader by the medical staff. Similarly, the physician should be able to "wear two hats" and constructively participate in the process in order to advance not just their practice, but also the service line as a whole. Ultimately, part of the role of the physician participants is to sell the strategic plans to their colleagues at the conclusion of the process. Thus, it is important to include physicians who are enthusiastic about the process and viewed as leaders within the service line.

Create a work plan

Developing a work plan at the outset of the project ensures that the process is structured and transparent. It provides participants with a road map of the steps needed to develop the plan. Given that the steering committee members include key leaders within the hospital and physicians, it is important for them to understand how their time is going to be utilized, as well as the timeline from vision development to implementation planning.

Typically, four to five meetings of the steering committee are needed to complete the planning process. The number of meetings varies depending on the magnitude of change being considered and the organizational culture. If the service line is contemplating transformational strategies, such as retooling the physician leadership structure or creating new programs, more meetings will likely be needed to discuss all implications, weigh the financial impact, and reach consensus. Similarly, the culture at each organization is different, and the process of facilitating the steering committee to reach a decision is unique to each hospital and may take more or less meetings, depending on the amount of discussion needed. The following outline represents a sample work plan:

- Meeting #1 – Discuss Project Work Plan and Objectives
    - Discuss project work plan and objectives
    - Finalize project scope
    - Seek steering committee member feedback

- Meeting #2 – Review Market Assessment and Key Interview Findings
    - Summarize project work plan and objectives
    - Present results of market assessment
    - Present key interview findings
    - Discuss potential working vision

- Meeting #3 – Draft Service Line Vision, Goals, and Structures
    - Finalize working vision
    - Define service line goals
    - Discuss potential service line management and leadership structures

- Meeting #4 – Develop Strategic Initiatives and Finalize Service Line Structures
    - Finalize CV service line vision and goals
    - Finalize preferred management and leadership structures
    - Develop and evaluate strategies
    - Facilitate discussion, prioritization, and selection of initiatives
    - Discuss tactical plan

- Meeting #5 – Finalize Strategies and Review Business Plan
    - Present finalized strategies
    - Present business plan
    - Discuss implementation timeline and designate accountabilities

Situational Assessment

The situational assessment is designed to provide a comprehensive picture of the service line's current position in the market, potential opportunities, and the challenges it may face going forward. To gain this robust understanding, it is necessary to look at the service line and its key constituents from both a quantitative and qualitative perspective. The key components include interview findings, internal and external assessments, and finally a strengths, weaknesses, opportunities, and threats (SWOT) analysis that details key implications to the strategic planning process.

The interview process

The first step in any strategic planning process is to gain perspective on the key issues. This can be done through a number of means, but the most effective is interviews because they provide an interactive forum for gathering information. Interviews are particularly effective if they are conducted by a third party to allow for confidentiality and create an environment where participants feel free to openly share their viewpoints. Whether you use an outside consultant or a member of administration not intimately involved in the service line, the interviewer should be able to create an environment where those being interviewed feel free to voice their true opinions.

The goal of the interview process is to begin to understand the issues facing the service line. Key themes often emerge concerning the potential direction for the service line and critical success factors for the process. A secondary goal is to understand any biases of the key stakeholders and challenges that will need to be overcome to ensure the successful execution of the strategic plan. The interview findings, in conjunction with a data-driven analysis of the service line, will create a detailed picture of the current state of the CV program and its potential strengths and weaknesses.

Who should be interviewed?

Interviews are the time to gain a wide perspective of the service line as it stands now and how key stakeholders envision it in the future. Therefore, interviewing a broad base of individuals is important to gain a comprehensive perspective. All steering committee members should be interviewed. Their perspectives will help shape the process, and their biases will need to be taken into account when facilitating discussions. Senior hospital leadership should also be interviewed; they will provide perspective on how the CV service line fits into their overall vision for the hospital, as well as if there are any "out of bounds" areas that should not be considered as part of the strategic planning process. Managers of key areas, including departmental heads and nursing leaders, can provide an "on the ground" perspective of the operational challenges that are currently being faced, as well as potential resource requirements. Physicians from all constituencies should also be included. Their input is helpful not only in understanding their goals and concerns, but also in garnering information about patient care trends. In addition to cardiac care providers, a sample of primary care physicians also should be included in the interview group, to better understand the perspectives of referring physicians.

 Strategies for Superior Cardiovascular Service Line Performance

SAMPLE INTERVIEW GUIDE

Questions can easily be retooled to be more appropriate for interviews with members of hospital administration.

Introduction

- The objective of this project is to develop a CV service line strategy and business plan that will define the direction, scope, and resource requirements of a well-positioned, differentiated, and clinically integrated program.

- The purpose of the interviews is to:

  - Identify perceptions and perspectives regarding developing a CV service line strategy.

  - Understand current relationships and dynamics.

  - Gain perspectives on the strategic opportunities currently available.

  - All interviews will be kept confidential.

Background Information

- Please give a brief description of your educational and clinical background.

- Do you have any administrative roles at the hospital?

- Please describe your practice in terms of the number of physicians, specialties, and in-office ancillaries offered.

- Where do you have hospital privileges?

- What percentage of your clinical volume is derived from activities at the hospital?

- Have any physicians recently joined or left your practice? Are you currently recruiting?

- What do you perceive as the opportunities for your practice in the market area?

SAMPLE INTERVIEW GUIDE (CONT.)

Medical Staff Relations

- How would you characterize the current relationship between hospital administration and the medical staff?

- How would you characterize the current relationships between the various cardiology groups? Between the cardiologists and CV surgeons? Between the various cardiology/cardiac surgery subspecialties?

- Has the hospital historically provided all the resources that you have requested?

- How can the hospital better enhance its relationship with you?

Strategic Goals

- What is your vision for CV services at the hospital for the next five years?
  - Clinical quality
  - Programmatic scope
  - Differentiation
  - Growth
  - Patient experience
  - Physician alignment

- From your perspective, what is the gap between the current state of CV services at the hospital and your vision?

- What are the attributes (good and bad) of the hospital, and specifically the hospital's CV services, that differentiate it from competing hospitals in the eyes of physicians? In the eyes of patients?

- What would you hope to achieve through the creation of a CV service line at the hospital (if not already in place)?

 Strategies for Superior Cardiovascular Service Line Performance

SAMPLE INTERVIEW GUIDE (CONT.)

- – Increased coordination of care

- – Greater patient volumes

- – Differentiation of services

- – Increased focus and dedicated resources for CV services

- – Greater physician involvement in decision-making

- – Other

- Are there any technology or facility changes that the hospital should consider to better support a CV service line?

- How can the hospital best leverage its employed cardiology physicians to support and grow a CV service line (if applicable)?

- As the hospital considers opportunities for expanding CV services in the service area, what specific markets should it explore, and how should it seek to attract patients and physicians?

- What obstacles will have to be overcome as CV services continue to grow?

Governance and Management

- What role would you like to see physicians play in the governance and management of the CV service line going forward?

- Are any changes needed to service line governance and management from your perspective?

Closing

- Do you have any questions or comments on issues that we did not cover?

Analyzing the data

Spending time analyzing data is important to cement the plan in a basis of fact and to understand both the history of the program and where the service line currently stands within the broader market. The goal of the internal assessment is to analyze available hospital service line goals to understand what is currently working well, as well as internal challenges that need to be overcome as various strategies are considered. The external analysis firmly seats the hospital service line within the broader context of the market, highlighting areas of opportunity and potential competitive threats.

Internal assessment

Typically, the internal assessment looks at several broad categories of data, namely volume, financial performance, operational efficiency, and quality/outcomes management. Analyzing approximately three years of data can help identify trends and the impact of key initiatives. To make the data meaningful, it is important to identify the parameters of the service line up front. On the inpatient (IP) side, this means reaching agreement on the diagnosis-related groups (DRG) that compose the CV service line. This DRG listing should then be applied methodically to all data (internal and external). Some of the most compelling analyses are developed through applying a secondary sub–service line filter. For example, look beyond cardiac surgery and focus on coronary artery bypass graft, valves, etc. Hone in on sub–service lines such as congestive heart failure (CHF), electrophysiology (EP), and arrhythmia instead of cardiology alone.

The following broad outline includes the types of analyses that may aid in highlighting key internal trends.

SAMPLE INTERNAL ASSESSMENT

Volume

- **Historical Service Line IP Volume Trends** – Charts or graphs showing volume trends by service line sector (e.g., cardiology, cardiac surgery, vascular surgery) for the three most recent years.

- **Historical Sub–Service Line IP Volume Trends** – Charts or graphs showing volume trends by sub–service line (e.g., EP, percutaneous coronary intervention [PCI], CHF) for the three most recent years.

- **Historical Outpatient (OP) Volume Trends** – Charts or graphs showing volume trends by key area (e.g., diagnostic caths, PCIs, stress testing) for the three most recent years.

- **Ratio of IP to OP Volumes** – Charts or graphs comparing IP and OP volumes for key areas such as diagnostic caths, EP procedures, etc.

- **Volume by Admitting or Procedural Physician** – Chart showing number of IP admissions by physician (taking into account usage of hospitalists, if applicable).

- **Patient Origin Map** – Map showing relative volume of cardiac IP admissions by patient ZIP code. A range of colors will denote where patient volume is centered.

Financial Trends

- **Payer Mix** – Pie chart showing payer mix for the three most recent years (CV-specific, if possible). It should include Medicare, Medicaid, self-pay, commercial, and other payers, grouped in appropriate categories.

- **Contribution Margin by DRG** – Analysis of contribution margin by DRG for the most recent year.

- **Profitability of Service Line** – If available, analysis of the profitability of the service line, compared and contrasted over the three most recent years.

SAMPLE INTERNAL ASSESSMENT (CONT.)

Quality Trends

- *Quality Indicators* – Chart summarizing key quality indicators versus targeted benchmarks (e.g., door-to-balloon time, average length of stay, adherence with core measures).

- *Patient Satisfaction Scores* – Graph or chart showing key trends in patient satisfaction scores in the most critical areas for the past three periods during which data is available.

Operational Efficiency

- *CV OR Utilization* – Chart showing CV OR utilization compared to benchmarks for both normal and after hours (if applicable).

- *Cath Lab Efficiency* – Chart showing efficiency and turnover of cath labs compared to benchmarks.

- *Staffing Levels* – Analysis of staffing levels and key nursing and staffing metrics for the three most recent years.

- *Staff Satisfaction Scores* – Analysis of staff satisfaction scores for the three most recent available periods compared to targeted levels.

    Strategies for Superior Cardiovascular Service Line Performance

An analysis of research grants or resident/fellow satisfaction (if the facility engages in these academic activities) could also be considered.

External assessment

The external assessment provides insight into what the competition is doing and what differentiates the CV program within key service areas. This assessment requires defining the markets and then determining who are the key competitors within each market. The markets should be small enough that regional trends in care can be highlighted, but large enough that they represent relatively substantial volume. Defining a hospital's market in a meaningful way is not solely a quantitative process; it requires looking at where key competitors derive the bulk of their volume, as well as geography and roads that may impact patient care-seeking behavior. In a service area that is broken into multiple markets, key competitors will likely vary across each market. In this case, it is necessary to hone in on the programs with a true market presence.

In most states, an agency of the state or the state hospital association can provide a database of DRG-level volume data for all hospitals practicing within the state. The availability of this data and the degree of detail provided varies by state, and there are often some caveats around how the data has been collected and analyzed.

Typically, the external assessment looks at industry, demographic, and market trends, as outlined next.

SAMPLE EXTERNAL ASSESSMENT

Industry Trends

- *Reimbursement Projections* – Analysis of likely trends in physician and hospital reimbursement over the coming years given healthcare reform, Centers for Medicare & Medicaid policy, changing care models, etc.

- *Innovative Technology/Procedures* – Discussion of the forecasted trends in procedures and available technology and how they will impact the provision of clinical care and growth of the market.

- *Hospital/Physician Relationship* – Analysis of emerging trends in the relationship and alignment models between hospitals and physicians and how they will impact the market place.

Demographic Trends

- *Forecasted Population Change* – Table showing the forecasted change in population in the next five years, breaking out key age cohorts.

- *Map of Current Population* – Color-coded map showing the current population by ZIP code (for instance, darker colors may be used to delineate areas with higher population density). Include markers indicating location of competing facilities.

- *Map Depicting Population Change* – Map showing the anticipated amount of population growth/reduction by ZIP code. A range of colors should be used to reflect the amount of population growth versus decline.

Market Trends

- *Market Size* – Chart showing the total number of IP CV cases in each of the key markets for the past three years.

SAMPLE EXTERNAL ASSESSMENT (CONT.)

- *IP Market Share Comparison Trends* – Line graphs showing IP cardiology market share for the three most recent years, by service line (e.g., cardiology, cardiac surgery, vascular surgery) for all key competitors.

- *IP Market Share Comparison Trends by Region* – Graphs comparing key competitors' market shares by geographical region for the three most recent years.

- *IP Market Share by Sub–Service Line* – Graphs comparing all major competitors by sub–service line for each service area for the three most recent years.

- *Competitor Volume Maps* – Maps for top competitors depicting volume of cases by patient origin. A range of colors should be used to denote where patient volume is centered.

Lessons learned

Experience has shown that the following key issues can be critical in ensuring that the data is accurate, the analysis is sound, and the resulting assessment resonates with key stakeholders:

- **Define the market and clarify with key stakeholders.** Choosing the right market is critical to ensuring that the data tells a story. If the market is defined too broadly, it is difficult to differentiate trends and understand the hospital's competitive position in key geographic areas. If it is defined too narrowly, it doesn't capture the majority of patients served. The key is to break the market into clear, distinguishable regions, looking at patient migration trends, barriers to obtaining care, and geographic factors. Then, be sure that the leadership team is in agreement so that the finished product is not questioned.

- **Utilize a common CV service line DRG definition.** For the data to be comparable between both internal and market data, a common DRG definition must be used. The DRG definition should be broken into meaningful sub–service lines so that differences in volumes and market share across the gamut of CV services can be analyzed.

- **Understand potential weaknesses in publicly available market share data.** The market share data gathered by each state is different, and it is important to understand the limitations in order to appropriately utilize the data. Questions to ask include: Are all hospitals required to submit IP data? Do for-profit hospitals and ambulatory surgery centers submit data as well? Are patients originating from ZIP codes outside

 Strategies for Superior Cardiovascular Service Line Performance

of the state included? Is the data scrubbed before it is included in the database? These issues must be understood before basing key management decisions on the assessment.

- **Make the data tell a story.** Marry the quantitative analysis with the qualitative findings to understand nuances of the market. This illuminates potential problems with the data, and more importantly, it provides the insight on the market needed to determine opportunities and threats. Changes in market share combined with the opening of new facilities or changes in physician employment can signal the effectiveness of competitors' strategies. Fit the pieces of the puzzle together to make the analysis meaningful, and not just graphs and charts on a page.

Putting it together

The final component of any situational assessment is understanding the implications. Whether this takes the form of a SWOT analysis or a summary of key findings, it is important to highlight the key takeaways to make sense of the data and provide insight into key factors that should be evaluated as the effectiveness of potential strategies is examined. The classic foursquare SWOT analysis is illustrated in Figure 2.2.

FIGURE 2.2

SAMPLE SWOT ANALYSIS	
Strengths	**Weaknesses**
<ul><li>Quality of care provided</li><li>Skill of physicians</li><li>Strong hospital leadership</li><li>Inception of the interventional cardiology program</li><li>Efficient patient transfers within the system</li><li>Strong presence in the market</li></ul>	<ul><li>Lack of physician alignment</li><li>Cardiologists not solely dedicated to the system</li><li>Suboptimal standardization of care</li><li>Patient leakage from the system</li><li>Capital limitations</li><li>Lack of a tertiary CV strategy</li></ul>
Opportunities	**Threats**
<ul><li>Work more collaboratively with the cardiologists</li><li>Develop a more integrated CV program within the system</li><li>Create a common patient experience</li><li>Explore the potential to secure surgical capabilities should the neighboring program fail</li><li>Expand the vascular program</li><li>Form a mutually beneficial agreement with a tertiary care partner</li><li>Leverage relationship with employed physicians</li></ul>	<ul><li>State limiting the ability to perform elective PCIs without surgical backup.</li><li>Changes to Certificate-of-Need regulations</li><li>Key competitors becoming more aggressive</li><li>Reimbursement climate changing the physician practice dynamics</li><li>Physician groups forming an affiliation with another program</li></ul>

     Strategies for Superior Cardiovascular Service Line Performance

Vision Development

At the foundation of any strategic plan is the vision for the organization's future. The organizational vision acts as a touchstone to guide leadership and the strategic planning effort. While the traditional one-line hospital vision statement is important as a concise statement of desired direction that can easily be communicated and remembered, it is limited in its power to describe the nuances of a complicated situation. In contrast, a working vision is a descriptive statement detailing five or six tenets that will guide management over the next five years. The benefit of taking a narrative form is that it can capture all key elements and paint a picture of what the vision for the organization will entail. The best visions are crafted by all stakeholders—administration, physicians, staff, and even patients—making the vision meaningful for all with a stake in the hospital's future.

SAMPLE WORKING VISION

Patient-Focused Care

- The patient will be the focal point of the CV service line.

- The mandate for quality is driven by an internal desire to excel at delivering high-quality, safe, and patient-centered care.

- Physicians, other clinical staff, and administration will work together to ensure that services will be organized and delivered in a manner that ensures the best patient experience possible.

- As such, each provider in the service line will strive to coordinate the delivery of services in a way that achieves optimal access to care, quality of care, personalized attention, and cost of providing care.

- All providers of care within the service line will come together to demonstrate to the public and all stakeholders that the CV service line is a national quality leader, as proven through its coordinated processes and outcomes.

SAMPLE WORKING VISION (CONT.)

- The hospital's CV services will strive to be recognized as a leader in healthcare quality, as measured by thought-leading quality organizations, through focusing on gathering data and measuring quality and cost outcomes.

Programmatic Growth

- The hospital continues to be dedicated to serving the local community, but it recognizes the need to grow both its services and its geographic reach to build volumes and enhance financial performance.

- As the hospital continues to expand its reach into new markets, the needs of its community will continue to be served by the high-quality care delivered with a personal touch that currently distinguishes the program.

- As outreach efforts are pursued, the hospital will look to maintain this grounding in the community, adapting its services to meet the needs of patients in other regions.

- Growth in patient volumes will be achieved by leveraging current relationships, differentiating the hospital in the marketplace, and expanding market presence.

- Expanding market presence will entail building stronger relationships with refer-ring physicians, as well as creating a brand that is differentiated in the minds of patients and referring physicians. This will enable the hospital's CV program to be seen as a destination service.

- Increasing patient volume will also aid in the recruitment and retention of physi-cians, ensuring that there is demand for their services and creating an environ-ment that is appealing for new physicians.

Comprehensive Program Scope

- The hospital remains committed to enhancing its regional leadership position in CV services by offering the breadth of services needed to both meet the needs of CV patients and differentiate itself in the market.

          Strategies for Superior Cardiovascular Service Line Performance

SAMPLE WORKING VISION (CONT.)

- Doing so entails a commitment to invest in related programs, services, and infra-structure.

- In the near future, the hospital will look to expand the services offered in additional clinical areas, including EP and peripheral vascular, to ensure that the program is comprehensive in scope.

- The hospital will also commit to making investments in the program to ensure that the CV service line remains competitive and innovative, providing the requisite facilities, infrastructure, and technology to achieve this goal.

Team-Driven, Coordinated Care

- The hospital will continue to build a collaborative work environment among providers and services, which will help to reinforce the culture of success.

- The hospital and the physicians understand the importance of their interdependent relationship; all have a shared respect for and responsibility to each other.

- The providers' desire to help the hospital succeed is amplified by their shared goals, strong work ethic, and dedication to growth of their practices.

- This collaborative team approach will allow for the development of a well-respected, powerful, and unified brand that aligns all stakeholders.

- This team-driven, coordinated approach to care will be realized, in part, through the continued development of standard protocols and processes in the IP and ambulatory setting.

- Another key element of the team-driven approach will manifest itself as a management and governance structure for the service line, which will include shared roles and responsibilities between the hospital and physicians.

Goals

The purpose of developing goals is to set the bar for what you would like the service line to achieve. Typically, strategic goals are tied to elements such as financial performance, physician relations, and coordination of services, and highlight the specific areas of anticipated growth and achievement. Examples of goals that may be contemplated include the following:

- Recognition from national quality/performance programs

- Achievement of specific quality targets and benchmarks

- Increase in market share in targeted areas/markets

- Improved coordination between hospitals in the region

- Increase in patient satisfaction scores

- Focus on outreach and affiliations

- Stronger, more aligned physician relationships

- Greater speed and ease of decision-making

Goals can be shown as a list, such as the one presented here, or more dynamically, as a grid. The goals grid is foursquare, similar to a SWOT analysis, which helps strategic planning participants think through not just what they would like to achieve, but also what they want to avoid, keep, and eliminate. A sample goals grid is shown in Figure 2.3.

FIGURE 2.3

SAMPLE GOALS GRID		
	Has	**Does Not Have**
Wants	**Preserve** • Clinical expertise • Quality of patient care • Program size and market presence • Strong reputation as part of the community • Focus on key initiatives, such as reducing door-to-balloon time • Shared responsibility for success of the program • Personalized attention to patients • Relationship and effective coordination with emergency medical services • Healthy physician/staff relationships • Strong, consensus-building hospital leadership • Strong nursing program	**Achieve** • Quality outcomes • Growth in volumes • More successful recruiting and retaining of new physicians • Comprehensive program scope • Strong residency and fellowship programs • Focus on outreach • Greater regional and national recognition • Shared governance structure with clear line of authority • Management structures that streamline decision-making • Increased access to innovative technology and capabilities
Does Not Want	**Eliminate** • Scheduling and patient access challenges • Operational impediments • Communication challenges between cardiologists and referring physicians • CV surgery referrals leaving the hospital	**Avoid** • Mentality of "defending turf" • Alienation of aligned community physicians • Exclusion of key stakeholders from the decision-making process • Ambiguous governance and management structure

Strategy Development

All of the work outlined previously lays the groundwork for the development of key strategies. At its heart, strategic planning is about resource allocation and determining what programs or initiatives will be the focus of the hospital's resources. A good strategy is grounded in the past, which is the reason for the situational assessment, but looks to the future, which is why the vision is at the apex of the strategic planning framework.

There are a number of ways to develop and evaluate strategies, and the right method is the one that encourages a thoughtful dialogue and seeks to ensure that the strategies will help the organization achieve its future vision. It is essential for the key stakeholders who are driving the strategic planning process to critically evaluate all potential strategies, to ascertain their implications and ensure their fit. Specifically, the following list includes the types of questions that should be asked:

- From a market perspective, which strategy will best allow us to grow market share and volumes?

- Operationally, will this strategy enable us to improve quality, service, and efficiency?

- Which scenario offers the best financial potential?

- Can we afford the investments in capital, physicians, and technology required to achieve this strategic scenario?

- Politically, are there barriers that will hinder us in achieving this scenario? Are they surmountable?

 Strategies for Superior Cardiovascular Service Line Performance

One of the biggest questions about any potential strategic plan that leadership needs to agree on is how "game changing" the strategies need to be. That is, does the organization need transformational or directional strategies? For a hospital that is facing grave issues with its medical staff or a sharp loss in volume, the answer is probably the former. Transformational strategies are those that seek to be disruptive to the market in order to shift current trends. They create significant change, both internally and, if successful, in the market. Other organizations are not looking for a sea change, but instead need to refocus and refine existing efforts. This could mean reevaluating the technological needs of the program, reinvigorating outreach efforts, or adding clinical scope to the service. A directional strategy is still powerful, but it does not have the level of change, or the level of risk, inherent in a transformational strategy. Understanding key stakeholders' expectations for the strategic plan and the level of change that it will create is important because one of the keys to successful execution is making sure that the plan is supported by hospital leadership.

Most strategies revolve around several basic themes. In nearly all regions, the markets are mature, and there is limited growth in the potential size of the market. Thus, the growth is driven by capturing additional market share from competitors. To do this, most organizations create focused strategies to differentiate themselves from their competitors in the eyes of patients and physicians. This may mean a focus on technology and being on the cutting edge, or it could mean focusing on outreach in growing communities or directly targeting a competitor's current strongholds. Other hospitals use facilities to differentiate themselves, focusing on creating an institute or heart hospital that contains the continuum of cardiac services and creates a physical presence in the community.

What all these market capture strategies have in common is taking advantage of opportunities in the market and allocating the resources to make it possible.

Within CV service line planning, another common strategy is around creating greater coordination of care. This makes sense given that this is one of the reasons that hospitals create a service line in the first place. Service line governance and management structures are a key part of this strategy. Dedicated service line management, often including physician leadership, drives accountability and creates an administrative focal point for CV services. A strong, inclusive governing body provides a forum for developing and implementing strategies while involving both physicians and administrative leaders. Other important facets of coordination of care are facilitating strong working relationships between physicians, staff, and nurses, and looking to create standardized processes and protocols to ensure a common and high-quality patient experience.

Physicians are at the heart of any strategic plan, or they should be. Thus, all good strategic plans address how the service line will create alignment with the physician base and use them as a resource. There is no one right answer as to how to create these relationships; instead, this process involves layering several strategies to create the type of physician relationships your organization needs. Part of this may entail creating economic alignment through employment, co-management agreements, or professional services agreements. It also may include elevating the roles of physicians in management and governance. The objective of these physician-related strategies should be focused on creating the types of physician relationships needed to drive service line growth and development and enable the hospital to attain its other strategies.

Tactical and Implementation Planning

If strategies address *what* the organization should do, then tactics address *how* it will be done. Tactics are the specific initiatives and action steps that will be taken in order to achieve the strategies. For instance, if one strategy is to enhance outreach efforts in important areas, the tactics would be analyzing the market, determining the key criteria for evaluating potential locations, determining the services that should be offered in each location, and developing a business plan. Tactics should be very concrete and granular enough to form the framework for an implementation plan.

The greatest failing of most strategic plans is in execution. Failure to appropriately implement a strategic plan has a more deleterious impact on the organization than simply the organization failing to move forward as planned. Key stakeholders who were involved with the process can become disenfranchised and frustrated that action was not taken and that time and effort were wasted. Most importantly, it gives the competition the chance to take advantage of this inaction to better position themselves in the market.

The main facets of a strong implementation plan are detailed action items, clearly delineated accountabilities, and an aggressive but realistic timeline for implementation. Figure 2.4 depicts a sample implementation plan.

FIGURE 2.4

SAMPLE IMPLEMENTATION PLAN

Strategy	Tactics	Action Items	Priority	Months 1–6	Months 6–12	Months 12–18
Drive Growth in Cardiology Through Focus on Patient Access	Establish and Further Develop Cardiology Outreach Clinics in Strategically Important Areas	Look to further cultivate relationships with private practice cardiology groups loyal to the hospital.	Immediate	▓		
		Determine new hospital affiliation opportunities, particularly in key strategic regions, such as to the west and south.	Immediate	▓		
		Fully leverage the new hospital affiliation to gain a stronger foothold in the southern markets.	Moderate			▓
		Explore enhancing hospital affiliations currently in place.	Ongoing	▓▓▓		
		Develop independent outreach locations in far western sections of the service area.	Long Term			▓
	Create Culture Focused on Customer Service	Address scheduling issues and improve patient access to ensure that referring physicians are able to have their patients seen in a timely manner.	Immediate	▓		
		Create a dedicated call-in number for referring physicians so that they can easily reach a cardiologist.	Immediate	▓		
		Incentivize physicians and staff to focus on improvements in communication and customer service, tying a portion of compensation to metrics that measure levels of customer service provided.	Moderate		▓	
		Promote customer service initiatives.	Ongoing	▓▓▓		
		Continue to monitor and measure patient satisfaction and other indicators of customer service performance.	Ongoing	▓▓▓		
	Create Stronger Relationships With PCPs	Leverage the presence of cardiologists in outreach areas to strengthen and form new relationships with outside PCPs.	Immediate	▓		
		Explore providing neonatology services under contract to other area hospitals.	Moderate		▓	
		Strategize and coordinate with the department of medicine to develop new initiatives.	Ongoing	▓▓▓		
		Work more collaboratively with hospital-employed specialists practicing at affiliated hospitals.	Ongoing	▓▓▓		
	Increase Patient Access in the Hospital Clinic	Improve call routing.	Immediate	▓		
		Hire an experienced cardiology director to address operational issues.	Immediate	▓		
		Explore extending clinic hours into the evenings, and adding Saturday hours.	Moderate		▓	
		Continue to implement recommendations from the operational improvement project.	Ongoing	▓▓▓		
Increase Surgical Volumes by Capitalizing on Market Opportunities	Prominently Market Program and Outcomes	Cultivate and benchmark outcomes data to be used in the campaign.	Immediate	▓		
		Develop marketing materials for referring physicians that highlight key aspects of patient care.	Immediate	▓		
		Review and update the Web site for cardiac services to emphasize the Heart Center concept and provide outcomes data for patients and families.	Immediate	▓		
		Create a dedicated position for a marketing/physician relations liaison (0.5–1.0 FTE) who both drives marketing campaigns and works with physicians to aid in personal marketing initiatives.	Immediate	▓		
		Focus on advertising physician-to-physician marketing, looking to physician leaders to reach out to referring physicians and their colleagues at other programs.	Ongoing	▓▓▓		
	Explore the Creation of Partnerships With Other Programs to Offer Surgical Services	Explore the opportunity to develop a creative arrangement for offering cardiac surgery services at other area hospitals.	Moderate		▓	
	Set the Stage for Capturing Regional Surgical Volume	Leverage cardiology outreach efforts.	Ongoing	▓▓▓		
		Recruit an additional nationally prominent cardiac surgeon.	Long Term			

Strategies for Superior Cardiovascular Service Line Performance

Conclusions

A good strategic planning process has the following characteristics:

- It involves key stakeholders, including physicians, in both the development and execution of the strategic plan

- There is a clear progression from vision to goals to strategies to tactics

- The plan is grounded in the realities of the market and the hospital's current position

- Attention is given to creating a common programmatic vision and goals, which detail the desired future direction for the program

- Strategies are actionable and highlight the key areas of focus going forward

- The management and governance structures needed to support the organization's strategic direction are put in place

- There is a detailed plan for implementation and a focus on execution

Creating Aligned Physician Relationships

Historically, most hospital/physician alignment has been characterized by a largely voluntary medical staff, and the relationships have been governed by the medical staff bylaws or rules. Physicians typically operate independently of hospitals, even to the extent of competing with hospitals for outpatient services. The strategic goals of the hospital are not necessarily aligned with the objectives of the private practice physicians either. But recent trends in reimbursement, healthcare legislation and regulation, and the consumer market are increasingly rendering such competitive relationships nonviable.

Reimbursement has been cut, making integration with hospitals more attractive, as the hospital is seen as a source of financial stability in the eyes of the physician. At the same time, public and private payers have moved toward value-based purchasing models, and patients increasingly demand access to a continuum of services through a single entry point. Patients also are starting to choose providers based on outcomes. Meeting these demands requires close physician alignment, which is necessary to attain service line strategic goals such as growth of services, coordination of care, and enhanced quality.

Hospital leaders have also learned that optimizing clinical services requires a close relationship with physicians, since they are critical in driving program growth and enhancement. Without physicians, the most brilliant service line strategy has little hope of success.

For a CV service line to achieve its potential as a unified and coordinated enterprise, it must develop enhanced hospital/physician relationships. Aligned CV service line relationships generally share the following key features:

- Economic incentives are created for physicians to support specific service line goals for growth, programmatic development, care coordination, quality improvement, and resource and supply chain management.

- Physicians play an active role in service line management and governance, which studies have shown improves service line performance overall.

- Hospital administration creates an efficient environment that enables an enhanced level of physician productivity.

- Open lines of communication are built between physicians and hospital administration, which results in building a greater degree of trust.

Aligning physicians who participate in CV services presents unique challenges. Relationships between and among cardiologists, CV surgeons, primary care physicians (PCP), anesthesiologists, and radiologists are complex and tenuous. The impact on these relationships—as well as their potential for disrupting or enhancing CV referral streams and revenues—should always be a top-of-mind consideration when developing both CV service line and system alignment strategies. Regulatory considerations, market conditions, and physician desires heavily influence the viability of certain alignment models. The solution that is right for noninvasive cardiologists may be different than what is needed for vascular surgeons, for example. Changing reimbursement trends clearly have an impact on the degree of financial risk that physicians are willing to bear and affect their willingness to consider employment. Market conditions and competitive forces also play a role. For example, if a large cardiology group sees its cross-town rival successfully engaging with a hospital in a co-management agreement, it could spur their desire to develop one as well. Generational issues also influence alignment models. For example, the value of work-life balance and attitudes toward working in a small private practice differ for those recently out of residency as compared to physicians who have been in practice for a number of years. All these factors drive the need for flexibility when developing physician alignment strategies.

While many cite the clinic model as embodied by the Mayo Clinic or the Cleveland Clinic as the epitome of hospital/physician alignment, for most hospitals this model is not possible given their circumstances. However, it is possible to attain similar levels of physician alignment in a community hospital or academic medical center setting. A number of tools are available for creating aligned relationships, including co-management, joint ventures, medical directorships, professional services arrangements (PSA), and employment. The right solution—meaning the one that creates the degree of physician alignment needed to attain the hospital's strategies—is typically accomplished by using a number of alignment models, layering and tailoring them as needed.

Regardless of the model, the goal of physician alignment is to shift physician loyalty and behavior to support service line and system goals. Hospitals that employ physicians and then think that the task of alignment has been accomplished are mistaken. Employment simply secures or stabilizes the supply of physicians; it does not necessarily create an environment where the clinicians start to care about CV services. Once you employ, the hard task of getting doctors to help drive service line success begins. Alignment strategies should focus on achieving the service line goals rather than on adopting a particular alignment model. Generally, a mixed and flexible approach to physician alignment is needed, as this will be more appealing to an array of physician objectives.

Physician Strategy Planning Process

The process for developing physician alignment strategies mirrors that for developing overall CV service line strategies. In fact, the two should be interrelated so that the physician alignment strategies are designed to create the types of relationships needed to achieve the service line's strategic goals. As with the overall strategy development process, there should be a clear progression from vision to goals to strategies to tactics. The way to ensure this is to employ a deliberate process to aid in the development of physician alignment strategies.

Understand the hospital's goals

While this would appear to be a foregone conclusion, often there is not a common understanding among hospital leadership on what they hope to accomplish through more aligned physician relationships and what types of alignment models should be considered. For example, the CEO may be envisioning employment as an option, while the chief financial officer prefers other options. Particularly in a system setting, there can be differences of opinion among the hospital's leadership. Thus, the first step is to have a meeting with all key administrative stakeholders to create a vision for what the optimal physician relationships look like and what they hope to accomplish. Getting the executive team on the same page with respect to the general parameters they will consider is often a value-added activity because managers want to have a united front in communicating to physicians. Most physicians are frustrated by hospital decision-making processes, so front-loading the decision on which models will be acceptable will allow physicians and executives to reach the end point sooner. Often some education is needed to create a common platform of understanding around the models available for physician alignment and their benefits and requirements. The outcome of this conversation does not need to be firm agreement on the specific models to be offered to physicians, but it does need to provide an overall direction for the kinds of relationships desired and the strategies to be considered.

Understand physicians' goals

The second step in the process is to have a focused dialogue with physicians to understand the chief challenges they are currently facing and what they hope to accomplish by having an enhanced relationship with the hospital. While one goal is often enhancing the practice's financial situation, the true objectives of the physicians are often much more nuanced. Assistance in recruiting, ensuring the long-term viability of the practice, or furnishing midlevel provider support could also be important to the physicians. It is also critical to understand whether the practice president is speaking for the practice as a whole, and whether there are varying opinions and perspectives among the individual physicians. The latter is often the case, which necessitates communicating directly with each physician in the practice to understand the varying goals and objectives. Each practice with which the hospital is seeking to align should be engaged in this dialogue to clearly articulate the unique issues and perspectives of each specialty and each group.

Narrow the options

The next step is for hospital administration to consider the goals and objectives of both parties and determine the options they would like to present to the physicians. This requires evaluating each alignment option using a set of criteria such as:

- Fit with overall hospital/system strategy
- Ability to accomplish service line goals
- Ability to meet physician objectives
- Financial implications, including one-time and ongoing expenses
- Administrative burden

The answers to these questions will help facilitate a dialogue among the executive team to determine what alignment models should be presented to physicians for their consideration.

Present models

The next step is to present physicians specific potential models for how they could better align with the hospital. Each model under consideration should be

Strategies for Superior Cardiovascular Service Line Performance

presented in terms of what it aims to accomplish overall, how it works, the potential financial implications, and the benefits and requirements. Discussing the specific issues related to governance, management, structure, operations, economics, and so forth will be critical to ensuring a complete understanding of the alternatives. Drafting a detailed conceptual model of the arrangement is often helpful as a communication mechanism but can also raise and resolve key issues. This is generally a narrative-type document with a degree of specificity and not a high-level PowerPoint-type document, which often leads to destructive ambiguity. Facilitating a conversation with the physicians over which models they would like to investigate further is the crucial component of this step.

Craft key terms

Based on the models to be pursued, the specific components of this step will differ. In all cases, it requires reaching consensus on key terms and receiving appropriate legal review. In the case of employment, a practice assessment and development of a term sheet is needed. If an enhanced medical directorship is chosen, the roles and responsibilities need to be outlined, as well as the time requirements and the salary. At the conclusion of this task, hospitals and physicians should be in a position to pursue the chosen model(s).

Implement model

With key terms in place, the next step is to close the deal. This may involve several iterations of the final document and shuttle diplomacy to make sure that all parties are in agreement. A task plan should be developed for ensuring that all key action items for successful implementation are addressed in a timely manner.

Measure and monitor success

The process does not end with the signing of a deal. The success of the models implemented should be measured and monitored to ensure that the hospital is accomplishing its goals and to understand whether any adjustments in the models are needed. CV services are a dynamic environment, so the types of aligned physician relationships used to support the CV program need to be adaptable and flexible. The only way this can be done is by continually monitoring performance to ensure that the goals and objectives of the alignment tactic are being met.

Key Considerations

Physician alignment models range from looser structures, such as part-time medical directorships that engage participants in a limited range of CV service line activities, to more comprehensive arrangements such as PSAs, co-management arrangements, and employment, which can deeply involve CV physicians in service line leadership, development, and operations. Figure 3.1 depicts a range of affiliation models.

The right alignment models are the ones that address the unique needs of both the service line and the physicians; they should align the goals and objectives of both parties. Often, this involves adopting and layering multiple models that meet the specific needs of individual physician groups or subspecialties, and revising them over time to address emerging needs.

    Strategies for Superior Cardiovascular Service Line Performance

FIGURE 3.1

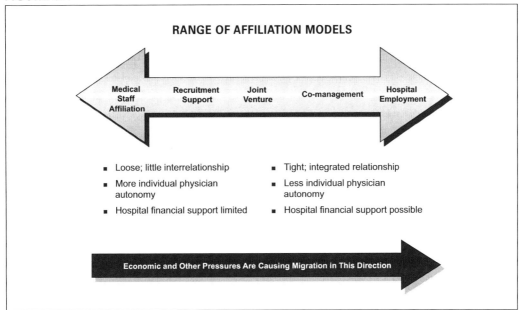

RANGE OF AFFILIATION MODELS

Medical Staff Affiliation — Recruitment Support — Joint Venture — Co-management — Hospital Employment

- Loose; little interrelationship
- More individual physician autonomy
- Hospital financial support limited

- Tight; integrated relationship
- Less individual physician autonomy
- Hospital financial support possible

Economic and Other Pressures Are Causing Migration in This Direction

When weighing the options for physician alignment models, the following are some key considerations:

- **Overall hospital/physician alignment strategy** – The CV service line physician strategy should not be developed in isolation, but should instead complement the hospital's overall strategies. The CV physician alignment strategy should be integrated with the overall hospital or system physician alignment strategy. If the system already has established physician alignment goals and models, these arrangements should guide the strategy for the CV service line, ensuring that there is a degree of consistency in how alignment is being pursued. However, since CV services are typically a large, if not the largest, contributor to a hospital's contribution margin, the CV service line may need to be at the forefront of other service lines when building new strategies and alignment models. Also, CV may be the first service line to develop a comprehensive alignment support structure, in part because its volume and potential financial returns can justify the large investments that may be required. In these cases, the CV service line physician strategy may serve as a template for other service lines or the entire hospital or system.

- **Analyze financial implications of alignment** – Large-scale alignment strategies may require significant up-front investments for legal services and transaction costs, and in the case of employment or comprehensive PSAs, infrastructure development. On the other hand, properly structured employment or contract arrangements may generate additional downstream system revenue. However, these gains are offset by physician compensation and practice operating costs. Any projected losses should be considered against the beneficial impact on CV service line strategy development and overall system revenues in the short, medium, and long term. For example, over a five-year period, the value of employment may be substantially higher than for less formal affiliations, even though the short-term returns are lower. Building the pro formas and understanding the business case and financial ramifications is important in deciding which alignment models are feasible and in forecasting any budgetary impacts.

- **Understand the impact on other physician relationships** – Which of the physicians will the alignment tactic encompass? What will be the reaction from the other members of the medical staff? If you are employing some but not all physicians, the CV service line risks alienating those

 Strategies for Superior Cardiovascular Service Line Performance

physicians who remain independent. Inviting representatives of all CV groups—employed, under contract, or independent—to participate in service line planning and governance, being transparent in all interactions, and developing clear guidelines for employment may mitigate this risk, making it possible to combine employment with other alignment strategies. None of these options eliminates the risk of disenfranchising the remaining independent physicians, which underscores the need for a thoughtful analysis. The need for transparency is critical in dealing with the political issues of a medical staff that is mixed with private and employed physicians. Therefore, many organizations do not use employment as a criterion in deciding who will be a program leader, medical director, or service chief. It is obviously easier to work in an environment where all physicians are either private or employed, but that situation is not a reality for most hospitals with CV programs.

• **Gain first-mover advantage** – CV physician alignment strategies may not produce an immediate bump in market share, but they may forestall your competitor from seeing one. Doing nothing and not focusing on physician relationships leaves the door open for the competition to take the lead and create new and enhanced relationships that may be difficult to reverse. At best, you will be pushed into quickly responding with a strategy that may not be as well thought out as you would like. At worst, you could lose critical physician services if you let a competitor move first. Whether it is being the first in the market to offer a co-management agreement or responding to physicians' desires for a physician/hospital organization, keeping a focus on physician alignment is key to maintaining and growing market share.

- **Prepare for reimbursement changes** – While the exact nature of the changes that will shape the reimbursement landscape is unknown, they are likely to include a shift toward bundled payments and pay for performance. Over the past several years, payment policy for Medicare patients has clearly put tremendous pressure on CV physician compensation, and we are likely to see continued erosion of physician compensation opportunities in the future, which will further drive physicians to seek the economic security they think hospitals should offer. Thus, in preparing for these changes in the intermediate to long term, it may make sense to focus on the more integrated alignment models, which will be able to adapt to these changes. Economic alignment and the ability to measure and monitor key quality metrics will likely be critical for preparing for reimbursement changes.

- **Be flexible** – Physician alignment is a moving target; as reimbursement, market, and technological changes continue, so will the needs of physicians and your hospital or system. In some cases, the most prudent strategy may be to implement alignment models that are functional and possible today, with the goal of moving toward more tightly integrated models in the future. One size does not fit all, because markets are different and the models you adopt will likely need to be frequently tailored to fit emerging physician and system alignment requirements. While flexibility is important to address physicians' concerns regarding compensation and control, a standardized approach to adopting alignment models will generally enhance further integration.

Models for Physician Alignment

Physician alignment models vary widely in their cost, the degree of physician integration they foster, and their strategic value to a hospital or healthcare system. Each model presents both benefits and risks. Meeting strategic needs, improving physician integration, and mitigating financial risk for both physicians and the hospital are key considerations when evaluating alignment models. See Figure 3.2 for an overview of some of the more common models, along with their strengths and weaknesses.

FIGURE 3.2

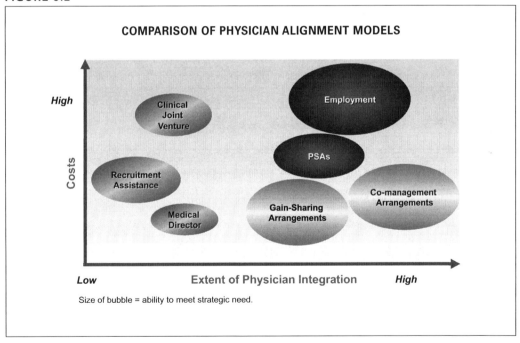

COMPARISON OF PHYSICIAN ALIGNMENT MODELS

Size of bubble = ability to meet strategic need.

Recruitment assistance

Hospitals have long offered independent physician groups recruiting assistance, primarily in the form of income guarantees for new physicians or aid
in the recruitment process. The medical staff development plan should be used
as a starting point for the determination of recruitment priorities and identification of practices for which recruitment assistance may be mutually beneficial.
Working with groups interested in recruiting, the hospital can then look to provide support in the recruiting process. If the hospital is able to demonstrate that
there is a deficit of physicians in a particular specialty via a community need
assessment, then the hospital can recruit and place a new physician into the
hospital's primary service area as defined for regulatory purposes and offer an
income guarantee. Income guarantees are typically structured as forgiving loans
with recourse back to the group or the recruited physician in the event the physician departs prior to fulfilling a multiyear service requirement. Alternatively,
the hospital can aid physician groups in the recruiting process by providing
help from hospital recruiters and giving candidates a welcoming experience.

The benefits of offering recruitment assistance are that it allows the hospital
to continue to support independent physicians and does not require the financial commitment of other, more hardwired options. Having a private practice
alternative enables new recruits to choose the environment in which they wish
to practice. Recruitment assistance may also help reinforce good relations with
the groups being assisted. An income guarantee also gives the independent physician group time to help build the practice of new physicians, shielding physician compensation while the new recruit cultivates his or her patient base.
Many groups do not find recruitment assistance enough to induce them to

      Strategies for Superior Cardiovascular Service Line Performance

recruit, however. Income guarantees typically extend for only the first two to three years of practice. After this time, the new physician must be able to support his/her own practice; otherwise, the economics of all physicians in the group are affected. Particularly in smaller groups, physicians face the concern that their income will be cut and their patient base cannibalized by adding an additional physician. While it may be in the strategic interest of the hospital to recruit to increase access to care and grow services, motivating private physician practices to do so can be difficult. As this demonstrates, fundamentally, recruitment assistance on its own does not necessarily align physician incentives with hospital incentives, so it generally has to be used in conjunction with other alignment tools.

Another issue with recruitment assistance is the current regulatory constraint on the group imposing restrictive covenants on the new physician. Groups are understandably reluctant to take on a new physician and help him or her establish a healthy practice if that physician has no restriction on competing with the group should things not work out. Another dilemma in recruiting arrangements is that the hospital cannot provide support to the group to cover incremental overhead costs unless those costs are new costs necessitated by a new physician. Consulting legal counsel regarding these restrictions, as well as the regulatory and legal issues regarding any alignment model, is warranted.

Placing the hospital-employed physician in an independent group

An attractive alternative to a recruiting arrangement is placing a new physician who has been hired by the hospital in an established medical practice. This is an advantage to the group because it avoids some of the regulatory constraints of the recruiting arrangement and allows the hospital to pay for the employed physician's use of space and other overhead items the physician uses in the practice. Also, in this type of arrangement, there is no recourse to the physician or the group if the physician leaves prior to fulfilling a service requirement, because these arrangements are structured as employment agreements. These arrangements allow the physician to build a practice within the envelope of the group and, in many instances, at the end of the employment period, the physician can join the group.

Medical directorships

Medical directorships are a very common means to involve physicians in hospital administrative roles. However, to be an effective physician alignment tool, they need to be carefully structured so the physician will have the proper incentives to attain hospital and service line goals. As physicians come under increasing reimbursement pressure, they are more likely to require compensation for participating in activities that were once considered voluntary medical staff duties, including medical staff administration, quality improvement, and peer review duties. Paying independent physicians as part-time medical directors to provide these services is one way to encourage participation and engage them in service line planning and management. Most hospitals have historically utilized medical directorships, such as chiefs of cardiology or cath lab directors, as a means to relate to physicians and perhaps to give them an alternate revenue stream. However, these relationships are being reexamined, both to ensure that the agreements meet legal requirements and to drive active participation in the service line. Medical directorships are being redesigned to include specific roles and responsibilities that enhance service line function and include incentive-based payments.

Under an enhanced medical director arrangement, physicians may become part-time employees of the hospital or remain as independent contractors for the portion of their time spent conducting medical directorship duties. Physicians are compensated based on fixed and variable components, with the variable components dependent on achievement of specific, targeted goals. Compensation is set in advance for the contract year and must meet fair market value (FMV) standards and not vary with the volume or value of referrals. Typically, the fixed component of the compensation is based on market levels of compensation for the physician's specialty, taking into account the time commitment required. The variable component is determined at the time of contract development based on mutual agreement by both parties, and again must comply with FMV standards.

- Specific roles and responsibilities for the fixed portion of the contract typically relate to:
    - Clinical oversight
    - Quality improvement initiatives
    - Involvement in hospital and service line committees
    - Providing leadership for strategic service line activities
- Specific metrics used to award the variable portion of the agreement could include:
    - Improvements in patient satisfaction scores

- Achievement of specific quality/outcomes management goals, such as improvements in patient outcomes and compliance with Centers for Medicare & Medicaid Services core measures

- Achievement of strategic programmatic goals, such as recruitment of new physicians, giving presentations to the community, and timely development of a new strategic plan within a specified time period

- Recognizing improvements in operational efficiency, such as enhanced clinical protocols

An advantage of paid medical directorships is that they can improve quality and care coordination through greater physician involvement in program design and oversight. The roles and responsibilities of medical directors usually leverage physicians' skill sets related to clinical expertise and programmatic development. Involving medical directors who are respected clinicians can improve compliance with new initiatives and drive support of service line strategies. Tailoring roles and responsibilities of medical directors to meet service line needs and using a compensation methodology that encompasses both fixed and variable components can help ensure that the hospital is seeing benefit from these positions. These directorships can also be implemented in a relatively short time frame with low start-up costs.

For physicians to succeed as medical directors, they need to be able to separate their position as leader of their medical group from their role as representative of the hospital. In other words, they need to be able to wear "two hats," which can be difficult for some physicians. Choosing medical directors can also be a highly politicized and polarizing process. Physicians from rival groups may see the appointment of a physician from the opposing group as a show of favoritism by the hospital. Changing and retooling existing directorships can also be difficult. Overall, medical directorships can be designed to be supportive of service line goals, but they represent an alignment tool that is best utilized in conjunction with other models of relationship building.

Professional services arrangement

A professional services arrangement is similar in structure to the foundation model that is frequently used in states (e.g., California) that restrict the employment of physicians. Typically, a group or groups of physicians are linked to a hospital through a PSA, which is a contract that requires specific clinical and perhaps administrative services for a specified level of remuneration. PSAs can be simple or elaborate, depending on the nature of the services provided under the arrangement.

Some organizations utilize a PSA model to mimic the economics of an employment type of arrangement when employment is not optimal, either due to corporate practices in the local jurisdiction or physicians' desire for more independence. The diagram in Figure 3.3 represents the typical structure.

PSAs are attractive because they create strong, coordinated relationships while preserving the physicians' independence. In some instances, they are the first step before employment. They are also flexible, in that the services covered and the terms involved can be tailored to fit the circumstances. On the downside, PSAs are often very complex documents that require time for proper

FIGURE 3.3

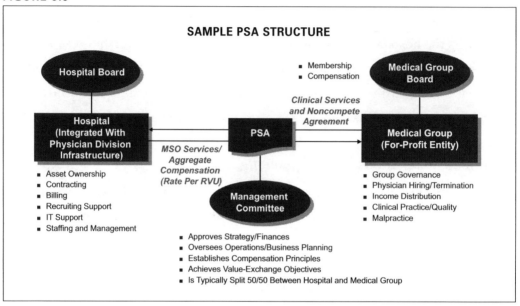

SAMPLE PSA STRUCTURE

setup and legal review. PSAs also require a degree of hospital infrastructure to be able to support and administer the contract. This type of vehicle is often chosen by organizations that want and are willing to invest in a tightly integrated physician group but face physician resistance to employment.

Gain-sharing arrangements

Office of Inspector General (OIG)–approved gain-sharing arrangements entail that the hospital share cost savings with associated physicians under an approved structure. Under these arrangements, the hospital pays the associated physicians a portion of the cost savings (historical costs less actual costs) directly attributable to specific changes in quality improvement. Payments are made to the physicians on a per capita basis. The hospital hires a program

Strategies for Superior Cardiovascular Service Line Performance

administrator to study historical practices and identify specific cost-saving opportunities. The hospital and physician review and adopt recommendations as medically appropriate. Cost savings are calculated separately for each recommendation to preclude shifting of cost savings. A "floor" is established for expected savings with no credit below the floor. There is no sharing of cost savings resulting from additional procedures, and extensions are expected to incorporate updated base-year costs. To satisfy requirements, there must be no steering of costly patients to other hospitals, and this must be monitored through study of case severity, ages, and payers. Also, the arrangement must be disclosed to patients, in writing.

The advantage of a gain-sharing arrangement is that it explicitly aligns physician and hospital financial incentives in pursuit of predetermined cost and quality goals. This promotes integration by directly involving physicians in determining the goals, making program improvements such as protocol adjustments to meet them, and holding physicians accountable for the results. It also is a step in preparing the hospital for value-based reimbursement trends.

However, gain-sharing arrangements have many disadvantages. One is that they are subject to close scrutiny by the OIG, which has approved only a few gain-sharing structures. Ensuring that a gain-sharing arrangement meets governmental requirements requires expert legal guidance, as well as administrative infrastructure to ensure that the metrics and measures are tracked and documented appropriately. Gain-sharing arrangements can also have limited appeal to physicians, because the metrics used are somewhat narrow in focus and may not provide the degree of economic support desired.

Equity joint ventures

Equity joint ventures are arrangements in which physicians and the hospital create a separate entity in which they both invest and hold ownership stakes to provide clinical equipment or services. As the name suggests, equity joint ventures involve selling physicians a share of an entity that earns technical revenue. The physicians' ownership position is often combined with significant physician control of day-to-day operations, staffing, and scheduling. If an existing business is converted to a joint venture, it must be purchased by the venture at FMV. The joint venture is governed by a board with representatives from both parties, and profits are split according to their respective ownership interests. Investors earn a return on their investment from both dividends and capital appreciation. The diagram in Figure 3.4 represents the typical structure of an equity joint venture.

FIGURE 3.4

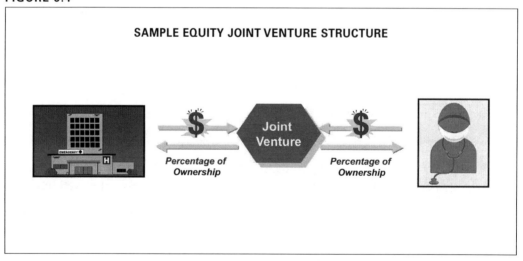

SAMPLE EQUITY JOINT VENTURE STRUCTURE

    Strategies for Superior Cardiovascular Service Line Performance

The chief benefit of a joint venture to the hospital is that through aligned incentives, it supports collaboration and trust between the hospital and physicians. It gives the two parties an opportunity to work together as business partners and enhance their relationship. Given that the returns from these arrangements can be sizable, it also provides a means to enhance the economics of the physicians' practice.

For physicians, an equity joint venture diversifies revenue and increases compensation. It can also secure a strong market advantage by making the hospital a partner instead of an adversary. Given that both parties have seats on the entity's board, it also gives the physicians a voice in the facility's operation.

Several challenges must be addressed with any joint venture and factored into the decision to enter a joint venture. First, for the hospital, it can represent a loss of hospital revenue, and increased volume from the new entity may not be sufficient to recover lost technical revenue. Reimbursement for outpatient services in a freestanding setting may also be lower, resulting in lower revenue than if identical procedures were performed in the hospital. That being said, effective communication with physicians, careful construction of the joint venture, and early inclusion of legal counsel can help to mitigate many of the common risks.

Co-management agreements

Under a co-management agreement, physicians and the hospital form a joint venture management company for the purpose of providing management services for the CV service line or specific elements of the service line, such as the cath lab. The management company works in conjunction with CV program administration to lead the service line and implement strategies. The management company enters into subcontracts with individual physician members to serve as medical directors and potentially employ the program administrator. The scope of the services required from program management determines the breadth of the management agreement and the fees associated with management services. The management company, through its designated physician leaders, provides administrative, medical director, and quality improvement services, as negotiated by the management company. The ownership of the management company and distributions are based on the capital contributed to the venture. Capitalized expenses, including a portion of start-up fees and the value of any equipment, are included in the company.

Functions of the new management company may include:

- Actively managing all vascular services operations

- Advising on and implementing measures to improve the quality of service

- Advising on and implementing operational efficiencies and performance improvement in the delivery of service

- Developing and implementing plans to enhance efficiency of resource use that would standardize supply chain elements and staffing

- Working with the hospital to establish and facilitate the creation of standard service line scorecards and evidence-based practice guidelines

A fee is paid to the management company, composed of a fixed portion and a performance-based portion. The management fee would be a fixed sum based on the FMV of standard services rendered. The performance-based portion would be a set amount, determined in advance at the beginning of each contract year, which would be paid based on meeting specific quality and efficiency goals (such as performance along core measures, adherence to prescription procedures, and increased patient satisfaction). It is worth noting that within the management company, there are no passive investors; all physician partners are expected to take an active leadership role or at least be active in the delivery of patient care.

A co-management arrangement is a joint venture between a hospital or system and a group of physicians that is charged with managing all or part of a CV service line. The co-management entity sets performance metrics for the service line and may employ or lease the service line administrator, medical directors, and other management and administrative personnel. The service line pays a fee to the co-management entity based on the FMV of management services, plus a bonus based on achievement of predetermined performance goals. The entity is governed by a board representing physicians and the hospital, and the profits are split in proportion to the ownership stakes of the shareholders. Figure 3.5 depicts a typical CV services co-management structure.

FIGURE 3.5

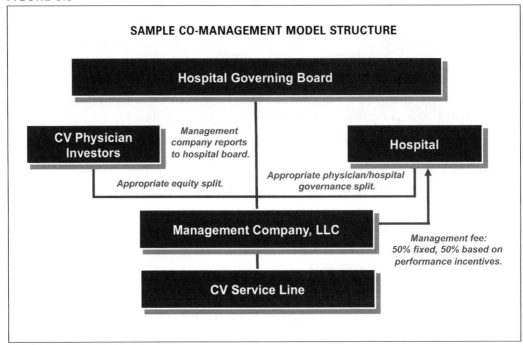

SAMPLE CO-MANAGEMENT MODEL STRUCTURE

A variation on the traditional co-management agreement is establishing a more limited agreement in which physicians aid in implementing select service line initiatives. Instead of establishing joint venture management of the CV service line, in this variation, the new company is tasked with implementing specific initiatives that leverage the physicians' skill set, and physicians receive an FMV payment for their services. For instance, the physicians could be tasked with developing standard-of-care protocols or exploring outreach opportunities. These initiatives should be strategic in nature and aid in achieving the service line's overall goals. The benefit of this is that it provides an opportunity to work together and understand whether it is something that the two parties would like to do on an expanded basis. Consulting arrangements for relevant services are generally straightforward and are typically limited in scope and of short duration.

The major benefit of co-management is that physicians become partners with the hospital in driving programmatic development. Also, in this structure physician managers are in a good position to enhance coordination of care. A great deal of control is ceded to the management company, giving it the ability to make significant positive changes. Financially, physicians can benefit from upside potential if they are able to achieve performance goals with the management company.

One of the key challenges is that a co-management agreement requires physicians to be willing to dedicate significant time to managing the service line, which affects their available time for patient care services. These agreements typically involve a large number of physicians; they may be difficult to implement with only a few physicians given the time commitment required. It can take six months or more to develop and implement a co-management agreement, and these agreements need to be carefully reviewed by legal counsel. Finally, implementing a co-management agreement may be more appropriate after the CV service line strategy has been developed.

Physician employment

Employment potentially gives the service line and system the most control and the greatest integration with physicians. However, employment is also flexible: it can be structured in many ways to achieve many ends. These include maintaining multiple small groups and creating subspecialty pods, cardiology institutes, or fully integrated multispecialty groups. Reimbursement arrangements with individual physicians in the groups can also range from productivity-based payment to methods that include incentives for participation in management, quality improvement, and care coordination activity.

When evaluating the option of employment, the following key issues need to be addressed:

Strategic

- Is employment part of a broader integration strategy, or is it a tactic to solve specific problems?
- How does employment complement other strategies regarding outreach, program development, and outpatient service development?
- How will the private medical staff respond to employment?
- Do local medical groups have the capacity and desire to recruit new physicians?
- For hospitals/systems with little or no employment experience, does the right infrastructure exist?

Tactical

- Is there a clear need for a physician in the community?
- Is employment the optimal solution, or can we provide recruitment support?
- Do the terms of employment ensure mutual success?

     Strategies for Superior Cardiovascular Service Line Performance

Employment is attractive to many CV physicians facing reimbursement cuts and higher operating costs. It also appeals to younger physicians, who generally seek a better work-life balance than their older colleagues. Increasingly, employment is becoming a practical necessity to keep physicians in place and recruit new physicians.

Employing CV physicians also presents a variety of challenges, including maintaining financial viability and risking alienating remaining nonemployed physicians. To fully integrate physicians with service line operations, employment also requires significant investment in practice management and support infrastructure, and the employed practice may never break even on operations. Because the financial and strategic risk are high, employment arrangements must be carefully structured to promote productivity and physician participation in service line governance.

Legal and Regulatory Considerations

The Anti-Kickback Statute and Stark Law must be considered when identifying and structuring joint venture opportunities. The Anti-Kickback Statute prohibits the giving or receiving of remuneration in return for goods or services reimbursable by Medicare or Medicaid. Stark Law prohibits the rendering of certain "designated health services" reimbursable under Medicare or Medicaid by entities that have a "financial relationship" with the patient's referring physician unless a regulatory exception is applicable. Established exceptions to the Stark Law permit many typical relationships between hospitals and physicians.

Given the complexity and ever-changing nature of the various laws and regulations that are implicated by hospital-physician economic relationships, it is important to consult legal counsel when structuring these arrangements.

Lessons Learned

Experience with top-performing CV programs across the country has yielded the following lessons for developing aligned physician relationships:

- Physician recruitment and alignment/relationship development need to become distinct competencies.

- Physician services are a distinct business and needs to be treated as such.

- Effective relationship structures hardwire communication and participation.

- A global plan for physician alignment needs to be developed that promulgates the hospital's mission, values, and strategy.

- Multiple initiatives typically need to be developed.

- Physicians, administration, and board members should be involved in the planning process.

- Infrastructure has to be built to operationalize the plan.

- Financial pressures facing physicians are likely to continue for some time, resulting in increased friction between and among PCPs, specialists, and healthcare systems.

   Strategies for Superior Cardiovascular Service Line Performance

- Most executives find it more effective to employ than align. However, this is something that needs to be determined by the senior leadership team. Set a strategy and follow it through.

- Strategies should be designed with flexibility in mind, because the balance of power between medical groups, hospitals, and other providers could change over time.

Building Optimal Management and Governance Constructs

The goal of a service line is to create a distinct, coordinated set of services that are recognizable as such to patients and care providers. Key to putting this concept into action is creating a unified management and governance structure that oversees operations of the services. Having dedicated service line management ensures that there is a single point of responsibility and accountability, which aids in coordinating the departments that comprise the service line, implementing key initiatives and planning efforts, and ensuring performance targets are met. An inclusive governance structure provides a forum for physicians from multiple groups and specialties to come together with members of administration to provide leadership for the service line. It both empowers the physicians and expedites decision-making.

Management Structures

In a typical departmental structure, each service reports to a departmental manager, who then reports to the chief operating officer (COO) or chief nursing officer (CNO). The cath lab manager reports to the director of patient care services, who then reports to the COO. The cardiac intensive care unit

(CICU) nurse manager reports to the director of inpatient nursing, who reports to the CNO. Such a structure creates a distinct hierarchy with clear spans of control. It does not, however, lend itself to coordination of care across the inpatient and outpatient arenas, nor does it facilitate cross-departmental strategic planning.

A service line management structure eliminates the vertical silos seen in the traditional organizational chart, instead focusing on creating an integrated structure with dedicated leadership over all cardiovascular-related departments. The benefit of a service-line-based management structure is that it can spur improved patient outcomes and higher-quality service because of greater coordination between the departments. It also improves the ability to execute strategic plans, thereby enhancing the organization's ability to increase volumes and drive market share growth. There is also an opportunity to better manage the business of the service line, improving margins and enhancing bottom-line financial performance.

In the evolution toward a consolidated service line, there is a range of models utilized in the market. Consider that the traditional model is fragmented, as shown in Figure 4.1, with no senior-level administrator and key departments that have separate reporting relationships.

 Strategies for Superior Cardiovascular Service Line Performance

FIGURE 4.1

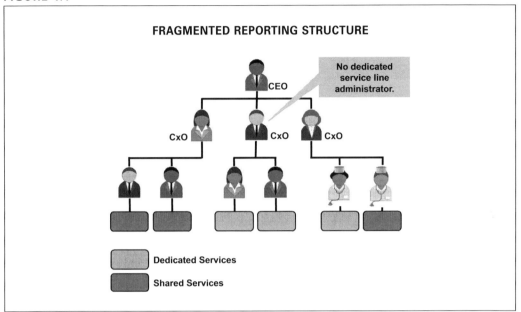

FRAGMENTED REPORTING STRUCTURE

The next step away from a fragmented service line structure is a matrixed reporting structure (Figure 4.2). A position for a service line leader is created, but this individual has no direct responsibilities for the departments that compose the service line. Instead, he or she has relationships with the directors of the key departments and advisory relationships, rather than oversight. While this model begins to create a service line focus, the administrator is operating in an environment in which he or she is facilitating efforts but has no direct control. This structure can cause delays in the decision-making process as multiple parties need to be consulted before key decisions are made. Further, success of these matrixed reporting structures is greatly dependent upon the individuals in the various roles working well together.

FIGURE 4.2

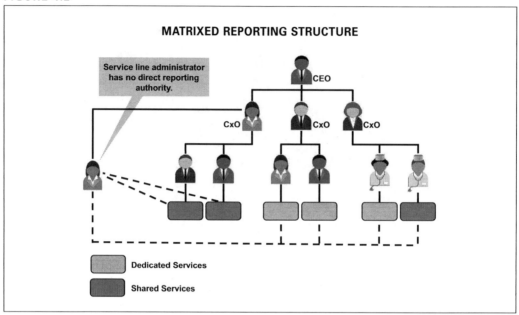

A partially consolidated structure, depicted in Figure 4.3, features a service line leader who has direct responsibility for some, but not all, key departments. He or she has a matrixed relationship with those departments that do not fall under the purview of the service line. For example, under this structure, the service line leader would have the cath lab and noninvasive testing functions reporting to him or her, but would have a matrixed relationship with the director of surgery for CV surgery functions. Such frameworks are common when political barriers exist to changing the control structure for key departments or services. A partially consolidated structure can work efficiently, particularly if most key departments are centralized under service line management and there are strong working relationships with other key directors.

   Strategies for Superior Cardiovascular Service Line Performance

FIGURE 4.3

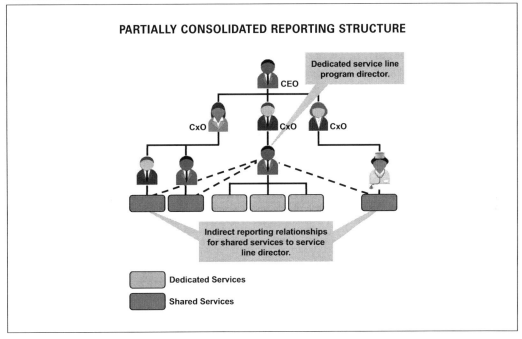

PARTIALLY CONSOLIDATED REPORTING STRUCTURE

In a fully integrated reporting structure, which represents the most consolidated and efficient service line structure, all CV-related functions report directly to service line leadership (Figure 4.4). In some organizations, nursing functions report indirectly to the CNO to maintain a line of sight across all nursing areas. A fully integrated structure streamlines decision-making, puts an emphasis on coordination of care, and enables successful execution of strategic initiatives. It can be a demanding position, however, given the number of functions and staff reporting to this person, and it requires an experienced candidate with a range of skill sets.

FIGURE 4.4

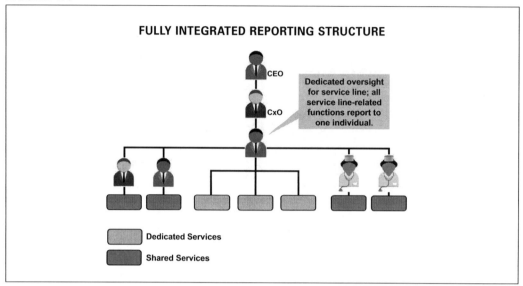

FULLY INTEGRATED REPORTING STRUCTURE

Service Line Leadership Structures

Management of the CV service line can be provided by a physician, an administrator, or a combination of the two. In recent years, many hospitals have begun to favor the physician-directed or dyad management structures where a physician is paired with an administrative leader. One of the key goals of better-performing hospitals is to create alignment with its physicians. The physician-directed or dyad management model is powerful because it elevates the role of the physician, driving alignment. Each model has its advantages and disadvantages, however, and while a leadership model with a physician executive is optimal in many respects, there is not a one-size-fits-all structure. Instead, a model must be tailored to meet the organization's unique needs. The benefits and requirements of each leadership structure are weighed in Figure 4.5.

  Strategies for Superior Cardiovascular Service Line Performance

FIGURE 4.5

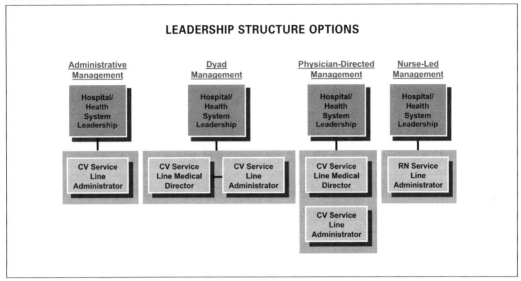

LEADERSHIP STRUCTURE OPTIONS

The administrator-led structure, which has traditionally been the most frequently used model, features a service line leader who understands the organizational, operational, and financial implications of running a successful service line from a business standpoint. The benefit of this model is that an experienced administrator may have a better grasp of the business aspects related to service line organization and development. The challenge for the administrator, however, is to determine how to engage with the medical staff in a meaningful way and to ensure clinical coordination.

The dyad model combines aspects of the administrator-led and physician-directed models, pairing an administrator and physician to work in tandem to lead the service line. This structure benefits by having both the clinical expertise of a physician and the business experience of an administrator. Also, it may create a more effective line of communication between administrative, medical, and nursing staff. However, there is a degree of added complexity that accompanies a dyad leadership structure because the roles and responsibilities of each of the leaders may not be clearly defined. The lack of a clear line of authority may also create inefficiencies.

The physician-directed model features a physician in the key leadership role, charged with providing management and clinical oversight of the service line. A key benefit is that a physician leader may be best prepared to ensure quality and safety, achieve pay-for-performance goals, pursue service development opportunities, and foster relationships with the employed physicians and independent medical staff members. In addition, physicians have a unique understanding of the healthcare environment, which may result in improved patient outcomes and compliance. Given that many physician recruits are interested in leadership positions, it also may be easier to recruit top physician talent under this model. The requirement to make this model successful, however, is recruiting a physician leader who has business experience and understands the nuances of running a well-managed operation. There can also be tension with the other specialties within the service line, depending on whether the physician leader chosen is a cardiologist, cardiac surgeon, or vascular surgeon.

Last, the nurse-led model elevates an RN executive to the key service line leadership position. This model is most common in organizations with a strong nursing culture that would like to have a consolidated structure but culturally want to ensure that the inpatient units continue to report to a nurse. The benefit of this model is that the service line leader has a strong clinical focus and can maintain the nurse-to-nurse reporting relationships. It can be difficult to find a suitable candidate, however, who is an RN but also has the degree of business and management expertise needed to lead a complex service line. This model also does not create the physician alignment seen in the physician-directed or dyad models.

PURPOSE AND SCOPE OF THE CV SERVICE LINE MEDICAL DIRECTOR POSITION

The CV service line medical director, in partnership with the CV service line administrator, will be charged with providing overall direction, goal setting, and input to key strategic, clinical, and operational issues for the CV service line. Additional responsibilities and qualifications of the CV service line medical director are described next.

Duties

The CV service line medical director will work in conjunction with the CV service line administrator to provide vision, leadership, organization, and direction to the CV service line. This will include the following key duties:

- Fostering a culture of collaboration and teamwork

- Assisting in the strategic development of new clinical programs and the establishment of service line strategies and goals

- Implementing select strategies as tasked by the governance council

- Partnering with other medical directors to achieve mutual goals for the service line

- Managing physician relationships and enforcing CV service line administrative policies and guidelines among physicians

- Leading quality initiatives, including measurement and monitoring of key metrics and development of standardized protocols and policies

**PURPOSE AND SCOPE OF THE CV SERVICE LINE
MEDICAL DIRECTOR POSITION (CONT.)**

- Supporting and providing input to the CV service line administrator in managing operations

- Monitoring and assessing key CV service line performance metrics

Roles and Responsibilities

- Devotes a minimum of 0.2 FTEs (approximately eight hours per week) to role as CV service line medical director

- Is appointed by COO, with input from the CV service line governance council and CEO

- Has financial oversight responsibility for the CV service line

- Reports to the governance council and the COO

- Has his/her performance evaluated annually by a governance council subcommittee through a 360-degree review process

Educational and Work Experience Requirements

The CV service line medical director must be licensed or qualified for licensure to practice medicine in the state and be board-certified in his/her specialty. He/she should be a practicing physician in the community. Business management experience is encouraged. He/she should have direct or indirect staff management experience and possess medical staff leadership experience.

Nursing relationships

The optimal nursing reporting relationship structure is not as clear-cut as many of the other areas of service line structure, but is dependent on how well current relationships function and the magnitude of issues related to nursing that need to be addressed. A range of nursing relationships is used, and used successfully, to engage CV nursing units with the service line (see Figure 4.6). Consider it as a decision tree. If the organization has a strong nursing culture, has historically had direct reporting relationships to the CNO, or is not confronting quality or coordination-of-care issues, then it may be prudent for CV nursing to have an indirect reporting relationship to service line administration. Changing the nursing reporting relationship is one of the most politically and culturally difficult challenges for many organizations, so if there is not a strategic need to revise the structure, dramatic change might not be worthwhile. If there are major challenges that directly relate to nursing or nursing functions, such as broken chains of command, quality issues, or coordination-of-care problems, then there is a very good impetus to enact change. In such a situation, a direct relationship to the service line administrator may be important, with an indirect line of report to the CNO. In this scenario, other considerations would be if the organization needs to appoint a strong nursing leader within the service line, or if the administrator should be an RN. The correct answer is dependent on the organization and its strategic needs.

FIGURE 4.6

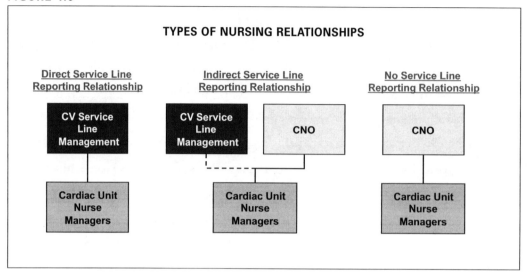

TYPES OF NURSING RELATIONSHIPS

Direct Service Line Reporting Relationship

Indirect Service Line Reporting Relationship

No Service Line Reporting Relationship

CV Service Line Management

CV Service Line Management — CNO

CNO

Cardiac Unit Nurse Managers

Cardiac Unit Nurse Managers

Cardiac Unit Nurse Managers

Governance Structures

The governance structure is the linchpin of the service line. It provides a forum for physicians and administration to come together to set the strategic direction for the service line and ensure performance expectations are met. Optimally, the governing body is an inclusive structure, with physician leadership from each specialty representing employed and private practice physicians. Key administrative leaders are involved as well. Roles and responsibilities are wide-ranging, including facilitating capital budgeting, driving business planning efforts, and maintaining accountability for service line performance. Typically, the governance body reports to the CEO or COO, which demonstrates the importance of this group and its role within the organization. It is

 Strategies for Superior Cardiovascular Service Line Performance

important to note that this structure does not represent governance in the classic sense, as it is subordinate to the CEO and board of directors, but it does provide a forum for communication and decision-making. Whether it goes by the name of a CV service line governing board, leadership council, or committee, it is crucial that it is not seen as simply an additional administrative meeting. This group plays a pivotal role in the service line.

This governance construct is extremely effective in demonstrating to physicians their role in the service line and the commitment of the hospital in having them actively involved. It also provides physicians with a strong voice and decision-making authority in effecting change in the service line, as well as overall guidance to the future direction of the CV program. The speed with which decisions can be made is also increased, as all key constituents are participating and can discuss and approve plans efficiently.

Committee membership

Membership of the service line governing council should be inclusive and represent all key constituents without becoming so large that decision-making is cumbersome. Typically, such a group has approximately 10 to 15 members, depending on services, medical staff makeup, and number of facilities included in the service line. When the group size exceeds the upper end of this range, it can be difficult to schedule meetings and facilitate decision-making, and the group becomes less efficient.

The council should have core members and ad hoc members, who are invited to attend meetings based on the topics slated to be discussed. Core members typically include the following (assuming a dyad leadership structure has been utilized):

- CV service line medical director, chair

- CV service line administrator

- CNO or designee

- COO or designee

- VP, business development

- Medical director, cardiology

- Medical director, cardiac surgery

- Medical director, vascular surgery

- Employed physician practice director (if applicable)

- Other physician representatives

The physicians appointed to this group vary based on the medical director structures at each hospital, the number of physician groups practicing at the facility, and which specialties have been included in the service line. If some of the physicians within the service line are employed, it is important that both employed and private practice physicians are included. This ensures that the group is representative, but, more importantly, it drives alignment with the private physicians, seeking their support for the service line strategies. Often a member of each of the key physician groups is represented on the council to promote communication and, more importantly, to give all constituents a voice in the service line. If there is an employed cardiac practice, it is important to have strong links between the service line and the employed physician enterprise, and the practice director should be included in governance activities.

Ad hoc committee members represent other constituents who are asked to attend council meetings as needed to provide their perspectives and input based on their expertise or role within the organization. Examples of potential ad hoc members include:

- Finance representative

- Other physicians, such as anesthesiologists, hospitalists, or primary care

- IT representative

- Marketing representative

- Physician liaison

- Other nursing representatives

- CV department managers

Roles and responsibilities

Key to making the governance structure effective is giving it power. Before the first meeting of the governing body is convened, the hospital leadership team must be in agreement on the level of control that will be granted to the group—specifically, budgetary influence. This concept gives many CEOs pause, as it seems to represent a fundamental change to the usual budgeting paradigm, but it is not that the established policies and procedures will be done away with. Instead, the council will be asked to develop a budget for CEO approval, and it then must make difficult resource-allocation choices and manage accordingly. Without a degree of authority over the budget, the governance council does not have the level of control and authority needed to execute on service line strategies, and the council could be viewed by physicians as simply an advisory committee.

Roles and responsibilities of the governing council vary depending on the level of control given to the group, but optimally they include the following functions:

- Act as the governing body of the CV service line, establishing the overall strategic direction and developing administrative policies and guidelines

- Establish the CV service line's strategic direction and supporting business plan:
    - Set and prioritize strategies for the CV service line
    - Develop administrative policies and guidelines
    - Oversee business planning and operational activities
    - Direct supporting committees
    - Review planning/implementation progress
    - Drive business development activities

- Oversee the budgeting process:
    - Work collaboratively with service line administration to develop the budget

 Strategies for Superior Cardiovascular Service Line Performance

- Prioritize key capital expenditures
- Provide input on key budget assumptions

- Maintain accountability for service line performance:
    - Monitor outcomes metrics
    - Facilitate operating and capital budgeting

- Review adoption of new technology/procedures

- Oversee quality programs

Potential subcommittee structures

Often, several subcommittees are used as work groups of the main governance committees, charged with addressing key areas of focus within the service line. The number of subcommittees should be kept at a minimum to reduce the number of meetings and administrative burden on key stakeholders. The subcommittees used depend on the most pressing issues facing the organization, but typical subcommittees include quality, finance/operations, business development/outreach, and research/teaching. Over time, the focus of the subcommittees can change to meet the needs of the service line. For example, if a new hospital or campus is under construction, then a facility planning subcommittee might be needed for the duration of the planning and moving process, but it would be disbanded or receive a new charge at the completion of the project.

The subcommittees should be viewed as the bodies charged with implementing and executing key strategies related to their area of focus, but they will always coordinate with the governance committee. For instance, the strategic plan may include an initiative for driving coordination of care throughout the service line. The quality and/or outcomes management subcommittee would then be charged by the governance committee to execute on this strategy and provide routine reports to the committee. Members of the subcommittee would meet; create a plan for exploring key tactics, such as building a dashboard of key metrics, creating standardized order sets, and utilizing patient navigators; and then report their continuing progress to the governing committee.

These subcommittees can also be used as a tool for communication, as well as to bring new issues to the attention of the governing committee. Subcommittee membership does not have to be limited to governing committee members but could include a committee member acting as chair, with other physicians and administrative leaders involved depending on the committee's area of focus. This creates broader involvement in governance and provides a means to disseminate information and to ensure that problems can percolate up through the system. For instance, the medical director for noninvasive testing could report to the quality subcommittee that there has been an issue with techs and nursing staff not being appropriately trained on a piece of new equipment. This would then be addressed in the subcommittee meeting, and the service line administrator and CNO would take appropriate action. Furthermore, this might point to an issue in the overall continuing education of staff and nurses, which could then be addressed by the governance committee. Figure 4.7 shows a sample governance structure.

 Strategies for Superior Cardiovascular Service Line Performance

FIGURE 4.7

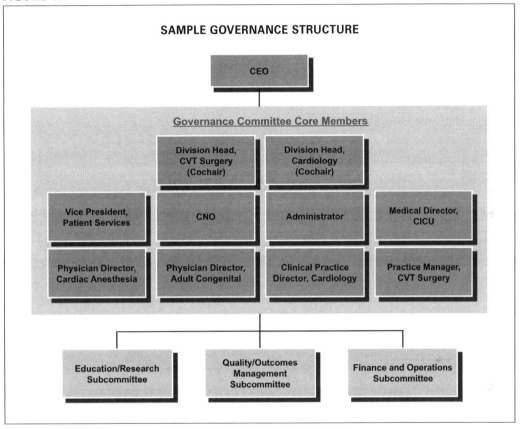

SAMPLE GOVERNANCE STRUCTURE

CEO

Governance Committee Core Members

Division Head, CVT Surgery (Cochair)

Division Head, Cardiology (Cochair)

Vice President, Patient Services

CNO

Administrator

Medical Director, CICU

Physician Director, Cardiac Anesthesia

Physician Director, Adult Congenital

Clinical Practice Director, Cardiology

Practice Manager, CVT Surgery

Education/Research Subcommittee

Quality/Outcomes Management Subcommittee

Finance and Operations Subcommittee

The key agenda items for the governance council should include standing meeting agenda items and critical strategic issues. Standing meeting agenda items to be presented at each meeting include a review of a dashboard of key metrics, reports from each of the subcommittees, and follow-up from questions from the last meeting. The bulk of the meeting should be devoted to discussing, providing input on, and reviewing key strategic initiatives. The initiatives to be discussed should flow from the annual strategic plan. To illustrate how the governance committee and subcommittees typically function, the following are sample meeting agendas.

Governance committee

- Review high-level performance dashboard

- Hear report from outreach subcommittee on strengths and weaknesses of potential opportunities, and prioritize new outreach sites

- Charge outreach subcommittee with designing business plan for next new site

- Discuss upcoming budget cycle and brainstorm potential capital needs

- Charge finance/operations subcommittee and administrator with composing first draft of budget

Quality/outcomes management subcommittee

- Determine key metrics to be monitored and presented at meetings

- Discuss additional technology or infrastructure needs to track metrics

- Review patient satisfaction data, and discuss key initiatives needed to target specific areas of improvement

- Discuss need to market key outcomes metrics, and charge select committee members with researching best practices at other programs

     Strategies for Superior Cardiovascular Service Line Performance

Outreach subcommittee

- Review performance of current outreach sites

- Discuss and prioritize areas for improvement at current clinic sites

- Prioritize three or four potential outreach sites to be explored further

- Charge select committee members and administrator in performing evaluation of potential outreach opportunities

- Discuss physician and staff recruitment needs to staff outreach sites, and develop recommendation

Finance and operations subcommittee

- Review key metrics indicative of service line performance

- Discuss highest-priority operational issues

- Charge administrator or designee in developing draft recommendation to address specific operational concerns

- Discuss upcoming budget cycle, and hear presentation describing the budgetary process

- Determine how finance/operations subcommittee can best interface in developing budge

System-Wide Service Lines

Creating a CV service line that spans multiple hospitals in a system presents both an opportunity and a challenge. The opportunity is the ability to work as a coordinated entity to manage resources and route patients within the system to the appropriate facility for care. This represents a tremendous opportunity for growth of services, enhanced coordination of care, and expense management. Political considerations make this challenging. Given that CV services are the largest contributor to the bottom line in many facilities, it is sometimes politically difficult to surrender control of these services. The degree of "systemness" currently in place magnifies this challenge. In fragmented systems of care, where each hospital operates relatively in isolation, the challenge of creating coordination between hospitals will be difficult to overcome. If the hospitals do have a precedent for allocating resources at a system level, these issues can be more easily resolved.

The overall goal of implementing a service line at a system level is to effectively capture patients and provide all care needed within the system. The management and governance structures are what allow this level of coordination to take place. In the case of a system composed of a tertiary care center and community hospitals, this means providing diagnostic testing at the lower-level facility, then routing the patients to the tertiary care facility for subspecialized care, such as electrophysiology procedures or cardiac surgery. Many of the same principles previously discussed apply, but they involve participants from each hospital. For management, this may mean creating a position of a VP of

 Strategies for Superior Cardiovascular Service Line Performance

cardiac services at the system level to ensure appropriate coordination, standardization, and resource allocations at all facilities. A key question that must be answered is: To what extent should the services be actively managed at a system level, versus by hospital site? In most cases, it makes sense to manage day-to-day operations at the hospital level, with high-level coordination provided by the system. Distances between hospitals and the level of services offered at each impact these choices. In terms of governance, participants from all hospitals must be involved. The governance committee then often reports to all CEOs or a designated CEO charged with leading the CV service line. Within a system, goals for the governance structure do not change, only the people involved and the individuals to whom the governing board reports.

One key for managing physician relationships in system organizations is that physicians relate to hospitals and not to systems. In a system of care, the physicians' primary point of reference is at the hospital level since this is where they see patients and conduct their service line activities. The system is an organizational construct that has little meaning to the day-to-day clinical affairs of a physician, so therefore relationship development will generally be more meaningful at the hospital level.

Service Line Development in Academic Medical Centers

Wayne Gretzky famously said, "Go where the puck is going, not where the puck has been." This statement is particularly applicable to the future of cardiovascular care as hospitals and academic medical centers (AMC) contemplate the design of a CV center or service line and the degree to which it is clinically and administratively integrated, including its medical staff. Organizations that choose a CV service line model with modest coordination among specialties that focuses more on branding and physical space than on an integrated care delivery model will be overshadowed by those that anticipate the changes occurring in CV care.

A convergence of factors, some positive and some negative, is causing the emergence of the new, highly integrated CV center and medical staff leadership model. Chief among these factors are the move toward value-based reimbursement, declining reimbursement rates, physician employment, and a renewed focus on public reporting of quality metrics. While the administrative leadership of hospitals cannot shape medicine or control these trends, it can take steps to reposition the enterprise and create innovative organizational models where the CV service line and physicians can thrive and deliver high-quality, integrated care. This will require assuming risk and in some cases making unpopular decisions that are in the best interest of patients and physicians. Today, organizations such as the Mayo Clinic, Cleveland Clinic, and Geisinger Health System frequently surface in discussions because they assumed such risks and created clinically integrated and patient-centric models.

Despite administrative efforts by hospitals and other organizations to influence the delivery of healthcare, it ultimately is shaped by medicine itself and those trained to deliver medical care. As depicted in the flowchart in Figure 5.1, medical education curriculum, approaches to training, and basic science and clinical research of CV disease will ultimately drive how AMCs, community hospitals/systems, and private practices organize themselves to deliver care. Organizations that recognize this and remain flexible, adapt to the changes in CV care, and create models that challenge the traditional boundaries by becoming patient-centered will prevail.

FIGURE 5.1

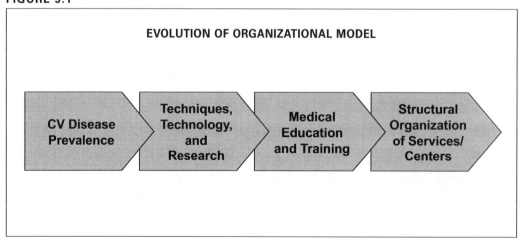

EVOLUTION OF ORGANIZATIONAL MODEL

CV Disease Prevalence

Techniques, Technology, and Research

Medical Education and Training

Structural Organization of Services/ Centers

        Strategies for Superior Cardiovascular Service Line Performance

Evolution of the Medical Staff Model

The history of medicine and why departments were originally created and how they have evolved provide insight regarding the future direction of CV services. Healthcare providers first became organized in 1518 with the birth of the Royal College of Physicians in London. Toward the end of the 19th century, "departmentalization" began to occur, as there was a pressing need to provide an organizational framework for larger groups of physicians, enhance communication, and share intellectual and physical resources, including space and equipment. An important objective of departments was to identify, recruit, and promote the most promising physician rather than allowing this important function to be assumed by others. These very same drivers of better program alignment and integration still exist today, particularly in CV care, where market forces have reduced the room for error and widened the gap between high- and under-performing programs.

Similar to what has occurred over the past several decades with the emergence of departments of neurosurgery, plastic surgery, and more recently, oncology, the concept of a department of CV medicine is beginning to emerge, encompassing adult cardiology, CV surgery, and in many cases, cardiac imaging. In numerous ways, the formation of hospital-based service lines may be seen as an administrative "fix" to coordinate care until training and other factors cause a fully integrated model to emerge. While there is renewed interest in service lines, centers of excellence, institutes, and the like, the concepts have existed for many decades. As shown in the charts in the upcoming figures, a natural evolution occurred in the creation of departments.[1] The understanding of how and why departments and service lines emerged provides valuable insight for organizations contemplating the way in which they structure their service lines/centers today. The pace at which CV care is progressing may suggest a more integrated structure, and anticipating future formations of new divisions or departments may be warranted.

In the 1950s, the organization of departments as well as divisions occurred in medical schools and teaching hospitals, driven by the need for more specialized training due in part to changes in technology. Furthermore, it was becoming too cumbersome to provide administrative support for an entire department, and physician and administrative leadership was warranted for smaller segments within the department structure. Thus, within each of the key departments, divisions with their own dedicated leaders emerged, as shown in Figure 5.2.

FIGURE 5.2

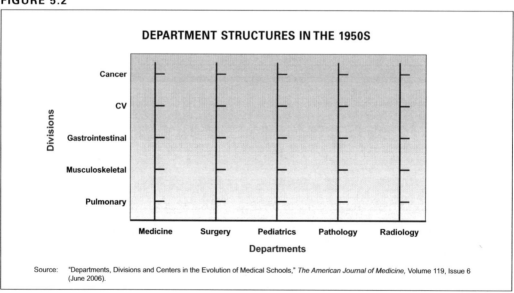

DEPARTMENT STRUCTURES IN THE 1950S

Source: "Departments, Divisions and Centers in the Evolution of Medical Schools," *The American Journal of Medicine*, Volume 119, Issue 6 (June 2006).

  Strategies for Superior Cardiovascular Service Line Performance

Loosely organized "affinity groups" emerged in the 1960s as the need arose for a multidisciplinary care approach that spanned multiple departments (see Figure 5.3). For example, the new specialty of cardiac surgery forced collaboration between surgeons and cardiologists and increasingly required the cooperation and involvement of CV radiologists, pathologists, and anesthesiologists. Such coordination was primarily driven by physicians, the changes in medicine, and the needs of the patients. The same tactics are being revisited today as the need for coordination among cardiac specialties grows.

FIGURE 5.3

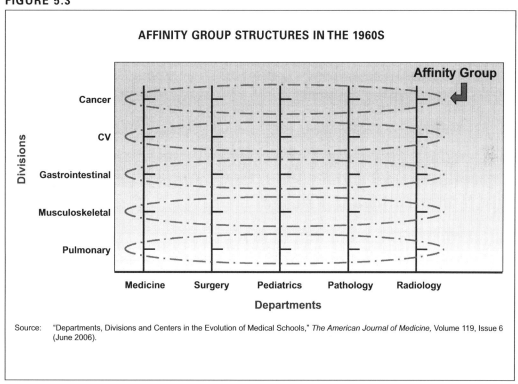

AFFINITY GROUP STRUCTURES IN THE 1960S

Source: "Departments, Divisions and Centers in the Evolution of Medical Schools," *The American Journal of Medicine,* Volume 119, Issue 6 (June 2006).

Centers, or variations thereof (including service lines), emerged in the 1990s, characterized by a more formal structure with dedicated resources and administrative infrastructure (see Figure 5.4). While there are characteristics and features that overlap, a center or institute typically encompasses all CV subspecialties and has dedicated resources and a formal governance structure beyond a designated management team. Service lines have traditionally been hospital-based and include at least two subspecialties with differing degrees of dedicated resources (e.g., staff and facilities). Despite the development of centers over 20 years ago at a number of the country's leading institutions, many hospitals are pursuing such models formally for the first time today.

FIGURE 5.4

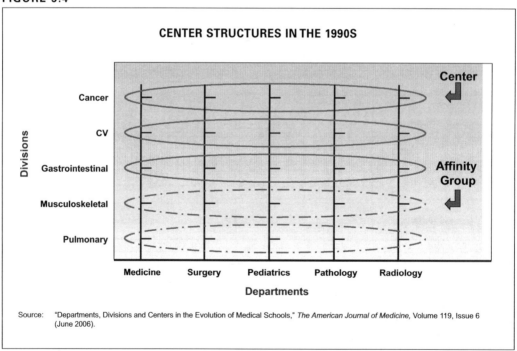

Source: "Departments, Divisions and Centers in the Evolution of Medical Schools," *The American Journal of Medicine*, Volume 119, Issue 6 (June 2006).

 Strategies for Superior Cardiovascular Service Line Performance

This is not to suggest that some hospitals are behind or at a disadvantage. Instead, it indicates that there likely is an opportunity to design a more integrated structure than originally contemplated when these concepts were first beta tested, and the situation provides the opportunity to create more integrated medical staff leadership structure. This potential development informs the governance and management structures, the role of physician leaders, and the financial model utilized.

Factors redefining relationships

As there were drivers that caused the evolution of departments, affinity groups, and centers over the years (as depicted earlier), there is a new set of factors that will continue to redefine and transform the organization of CV services and the medical staff leadership structure, beginning in the academic setting and ultimately becoming the standard practice of medicine for cardiologists and surgical specialists in the CV arena. The changes will likely initiate in AMCs as the academic departments and divisions modify training programs, which will in turn modify the way in which clinical divisions are organized in the practice plan and affiliated teaching hospital. Factors that will influence these changes include but are not limited to the following:

- **Technology** – In the 1880s, an adult cardiologist relied exclusively on his or her hands and stethoscopes. Today, within radiology alone there are many cutting-edge procedures and technologies available, such as cerebrovascular angiography and interventions, cardiac cine/ultrafast CT, cardiac MRI, gated radionuclide angiograms, vascular angiography and interventions, and vascular ultrasound. This is changing the skill set requirements of cardiologists (e.g., board-certified in both cardiology and radiology).

- **Medical Education and Training** – As shown in the evolution of departments, divisions, and centers presented earlier, medical education and specialized training will continue to shape CV specialists.

- **Quality and Cost** – CV care was the first major service line for which quality metrics were developed and are publicly reported today. This will likely intensify and will further force greater integration across the episode of care.

- **Physician Supply** – It will become more practical and financially feasible to train CV specialists to delivery multidisciplinary CV care, particularly considering the expected shortage of cardiologists relative to demand over the next 7 to 10 years.[2] Physicians will become more specialized and will train in multiple disciplines, reflecting the changes in medicine as well as growing expectations of patients.

- **Hospital Employment of Physicians** – With more and more physicians becoming employed by the hospital, greater economic alignment is achieved, which in turn provides the opportunity to develop new structures.

- **Internal Competition** – Internal competition among physicians, as evidenced by recent peripheral vascular turf wars, has been a hindering factor for organizations that aim to develop highly integrated care delivery models. The call for patient-centered care and quality reporting will further highlight the inefficiencies and other shortcomings of these antagonistic relationships.

    Strategies for Superior Cardiovascular Service Line Performance

- **Recruitment/Retention** – Hospitals that develop innovative care delivery models and administrative structures that are conducive to CV specialists will attract and retain talented physicians.

- **Healthcare/Payment Reform** – In addition to the natural demand for disease- and patient-centered CV care by consumers, payment reform will accelerate this effort through mechanisms such as bundled payments (i.e., accountable care organizations).

Pushing the Boundaries of CV Clinical Integration

While the factors listed earlier as well as other drivers make a compelling case for the administrative reorganization of CV services within an institution, the reality is that changes in medicine itself will gradually force these changes to occur, and it will only be a question of how quickly organizations adapt. As the standards of practice change, infrastructure and supportive systems will need to adapt accordingly. The factors listed previously underscore the need to reconfigure the traditional hospital department structure to eliminate unnecessary barriers that may otherwise exist between CV-related programs. In many of the current structures, the political challenges between cardiology and the division of CV surgery, for instance, limit the ability of the organization to achieve a multidisciplinary care delivery model. With medicine and technology driving the emergence of CV specialists, hospitals and other organizations will need to implement organizational models that are conducive to such a shift and remove the unnecessary barriers that may otherwise exist between CV-related programs. For example, technological developments have led to the now-familiar echocardiography, catheterization, and electrophysiology laboratories present in all major medical centers. Concomitantly, cardiologists have evolved to become echocardiographers, interventionalists, and electrophysiologists.[3]

For the past decade, there has been a call for greater clinical integration in CV care, but many organizations have waited for a burning platform to motivate change. The challenges facing CV care today—including reduced reimbursement, speeding the purchase of physician practices—create this urgent need for integrated care delivery models. Regardless of the impetus, hospitals should embrace the opportunity to develop a highly integrated model, tailored to meet the demands of the local market. Examples of attributes of a highly integrated CV model include:

- Dedicated, inclusive governance and management structures

- Integration financials (e.g., consolidated budget for CV services spanning inpatient and outpatient care)

- Colocation of healthcare facilities for patients' convenience

- Documented clinical pathways and standards of care, regardless of the entry point into the system

The coordination of care across multiple disciplines through a physician-driven model has become more common at a clinic level in CV services. These clinics may have designated medical directors and share clinical and administrative staff. However, achieving full integration across all points of access to CV care at a hospital or system level currently remains out of reach for many AMCs and community hospitals. The challenges primarily rest with the administrative, political, and economic requirements to develop more fully integrated models. The size and scale of an organization, number of programs, geographic distribution of the system, medical staff models, and presence of medical education and training programs can all play a role in determining the feasibility of implementing a highly integrated model of care.

The development of integrated programs within and among divisions or departments tends to require primarily the medical coordination of care and resembles the affinity groups discussed earlier. This could be described as "lateral integration," which is present in many institutions today and common in such areas as spine and digestive disease centers, as shown in Figure 5.5.[4] Lateral integration is the coordination across multiple departments and/or divisions for purposes of enhancing care delivery. This is accomplished primarily on a clinical basis with a common approach and protocol developed by physicians and clinical support staff with limited shared resources. Vertical integration requires a more formal consolidation and integration of resources from multiple departments, including administration and finance. Developing vertically integrated models in major service lines such as CV care is more challenging to accomplish, but if achieved, it brings the greatest focus to the disease and the patient. The Cleveland Clinic Miller Family Heart & Vascular Institute and Beth Israel Deaconess Medical Center's (BIDMC) CardioVascular Institute are examples of vertically integrated centers where clinical, research, and administrative resources, including physicians, are highly integrated into a single unit to deliver patient-centered care.

FIGURE 5.5

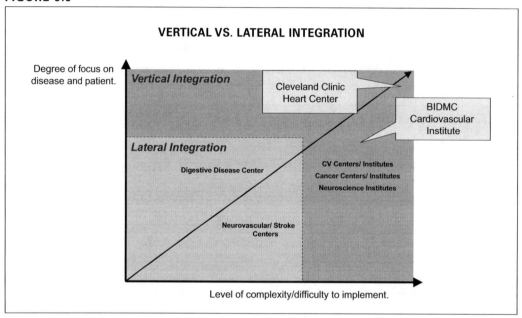

VERTICAL VS. LATERAL INTEGRATION

Degree of focus on disease and patient.

Vertical Integration

Cleveland Clinic Heart Center

BIDMC Cardiovascular Institute

Lateral Integration

Digestive Disease Center

CV Centers/ Institutes
Cancer Centers/ Institutes
Neuroscience Institutes

Neurovascular/ Stroke Centers

Level of complexity/difficulty to implement.

Revisiting the Departmental Structure

There is a growing possibility that in the long run, institutions will seek "full integration" and explore the possibility of forming a department structure. While this may not be applicable for some organizations (depending on size/scale, number of specialty programs, and relationship between the hospital and physician organizations), at many institutions it may be required for the organization to achieve its full potential. Modest efforts to further coordinate care among cardiologists, cardiac surgeons, vascular surgeons, and radiologists likely will not be sufficient to achieve truly integrated care that is focused on the patient. Some institutions, beginning with AMCs, are already

Strategies for Superior Cardiovascular Service Line Performance

testing the boundaries of integration and forming new departments for cardio-vascular medicine. As discussed earlier, while the conversion of surgical divisions, such as orthopedics, neurosurgery, and plastic surgery, into departments has occurred over the past 10–15 years, the creation of a department that draws from both medical and surgical specialties has largely gone untested. Nonetheless, we may see a progressive shift in that direction, and the creation of a highly integrated CV service line or center could be a prudent step in that direction. Presented in Figure 5.6 (at a macro level) is an example of an AMC's development of more specialized divisions across the system.

FIGURE 5.6

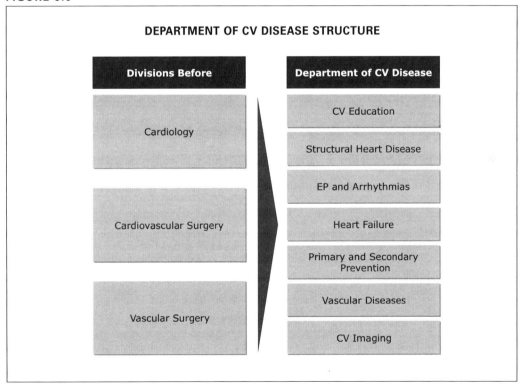

DEPARTMENT OF CV DISEASE STRUCTURE

Divisions Before	Department of CV Disease
Cardiology	CV Education
	Structural Heart Disease
	EP and Arrhythmias
Cardiovascular Surgery	Heart Failure
	Primary and Secondary Prevention
	Vascular Diseases
Vascular Surgery	CV Imaging

The traditional divisions within the medical school, faculty group practice, and affiliated teaching hospital were reorganized into a new department. This allowed for the creation of unconventional divisions and sections that are conducive to the subspecialty of care, technology, and changing needs of the patient. Equally important was the ability of the institution to refine its medical education curriculum and training programs to better prepare tomorrow's cardiovascular specialist.

Specifically, in this integrated model, the barriers between the departments are broken down and a department of CV disease is created, unifying all CV-related physicians under a common leadership structure. Figure 5.7 shows the organizational structures under a typical department structure, in which the chairs of medicine and surgery report through different departments.

FIGURE 5.7

TRADITIONAL DEPARTMENTAL MEDICAL STAFF LEADERSHIP STRUCTURE

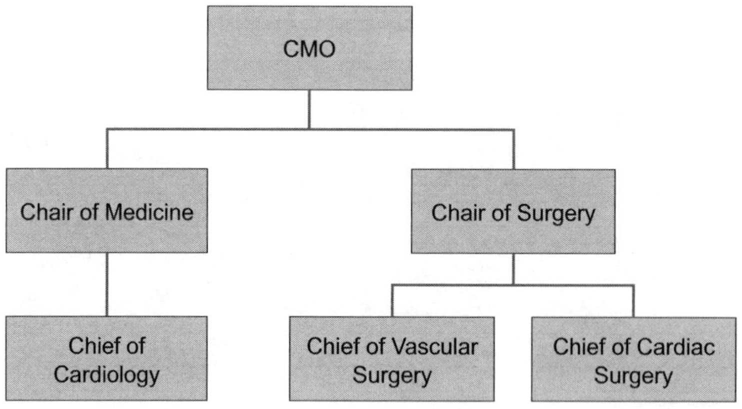

Under an integrated department of CV disease model, depicted in Figure 5.8, several key changes are implemented. First, a new position is created for a chair of CV disease, providing dedicated physician leadership. The reporting relationships are revised, and vascular surgery, cardiac surgery, and cardiology fall under the newly created chair of CV disease. While physician leadership would be centralized under the chair of CV disease, an inclusive governance council for the service line could still provide a forum for broader physician involvement in guiding the direction of the service line, including input and guidance from the chairs of medicine and surgery.

The benefit of this model is that it creates a more vertical and streamlined physician leadership structure, creating a single point of authority and account-ability, which drives integration. Fundamentally, it can enable the hospital and

FIGURE 5.8

DEPARTMENT OF CV DISEASE MEDICAL STAFF LEADERSHIP STRUCTURE

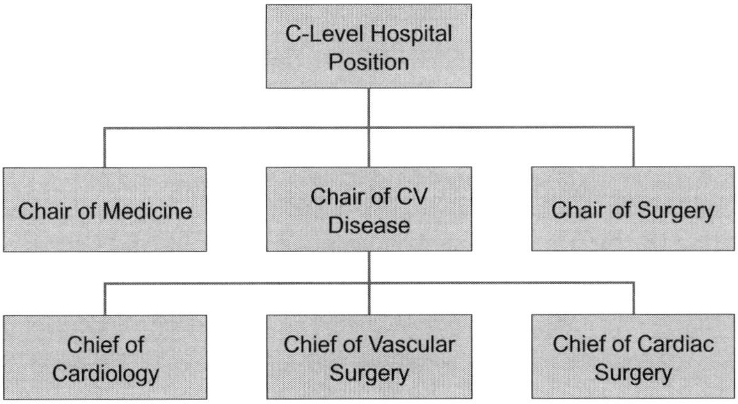

affiliated entities to more effectively implement measures in response to anticipated market changes, including changes in reimbursement, which may include
bundled payments for services. Additionally, reimbursement will likely be out-
comes-focused, as previously discussed. It also better replicates the patient experience, as patients need to be able to access the range of treatments for CV
disease without any barriers. This model also creates a streamlined structure for
all medical directors, with clear reporting relationships and responsibilities.
Meeting the changing demands of the market, it fosters more coordination and
collaboration between physicians of different specialties who provide CV care.
From a strategic perspective, it creates an enhanced focus on CV services, with
a clear strategic imperative for the service line leadership. As an innovative
approach, this structure may also be able to differentiate the CV program
within the market.

Change of this magnitude does not come without its challenges, and this
model is not optimal for every organization. Clearly it requires making fundamental changes to the current structures and lines of accountability, which can
be politically challenging. It also requires leadership from both the medical staff
and administration to be invested in the concept and willing to commit to the
change, even if not all physicians are on board. This model necessitates a single
point of leadership, which may or may not require the introduction of someone
from outside the organization who does not have political "baggage" and who
has experience with a similar model elsewhere. Choosing the right candidate for
this position can be challenging, and having a structured candidate evaluation
process is critical. From a graduate medical education standpoint, some of the
traditional departmental structures will need to remain in place.

This model, as presented here in concept, can be modified in a number of ways to best meet the dynamics of the organization and the demands on the structure. For instance, some of the existing peer review and credentialing roles can be maintained by the chairs of surgery and medicine. Matrixed relationships can be created between the chair of CV disease and the chairs of medicine and surgery. Responsibilities of the chair of CV disease can be tailored. The important concept behind this structure is creating a higher degree of integration among the physicians who provide CV care and creating an enhanced level of physician leadership.

New Physician Leadership and Team Requirements

As CV services become more integrated in medical education and training, it will place pressure on the clinical enterprise and challenge hospitals to modify their department structure and/or develop more integrated multidisciplinary centers. The differentiating factor for organizations that are able to adapt and implement more integrated CV models is the degree to which physicians are leading this transition. It is imperative that hospitals take an aggressive approach and assume a reasonable degree of risk to yield control to qualified physician leaders so that these leaders can design and implement governance, management, and operational structures to promote an integrated approach to CV care delivery. Too often today there is a failed attempt to accomplish this through a modest operations committee or a politically popular structure that involves a large number of physicians but lacks the wherewithal to make informed decisions. The push for vertical integration of physician leadership is not unique to CV, but change will begin with cornerstone service lines, and CV is at the top of this list because of the prominence of the service line and the money at stake.

The importance of having physician leadership driving the process can best be highlighted by the Cleveland Clinic. Delos M. Cosgrove, M.D., a cardiac surgeon who became CEO of the Cleveland Clinic in 2004, replaced departments with institutes that correspond to patients' conditions rather than an organizational unit aligned with a physician's specialty. This includes the heart and vascular institute, where cardiologists, cardiac surgeons, and vascular surgeons are united in their treatment of patients and where the measurement and reporting of quality is tracked and openly published. Too often organizations believe that institutions such as the Cleveland Clinic can accomplish such initiatives solely because of their history and reputation and the fact that they are already integrated. The reality is that an organization such as the Cleveland Clinic is constantly changing to adapt to the market, and the patient and clinical integration efforts continue. Execution is successful because of physician leadership.

Physician leaders are important, and will become increasingly so, in CV and other services across the hospital/health system in several areas, including but not limited to the following:

- Measurement, tracking, and reporting of quality

- Design and implementation of patient care improvement processes

- Integrated strategic planning for the service line

- Identification and prioritization of capital needs

- Staff education and development

- Supporting customer service culture changes

- Referring physician education, integration, and satisfaction initiatives

- Alignment and management of relationships between employed physicians and private affiliated practices of the hospital

The graphic in Figure 5.9 highlights the number of physician-led versus administrator-led programs within the *U.S. News & World Report* list of Best Heart & Heart Surgery Hospitals.

FIGURE 5.9

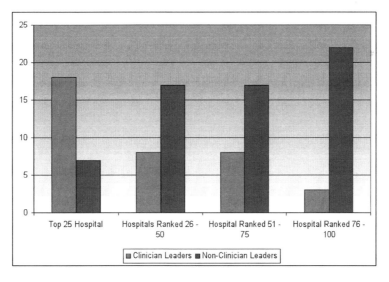

PROPORTION OF CLINICIANS AND NON-CLINICIAN MANAGERS AS CEOS IN THE TOP 100 U.S. HOSPITALS IN THE FIELD OF HEART AND HEART SURGERY BY QUARTILE

Data source: *U.S. News & World Report* Best Hospitals 2009–2010.

While this graph is not intended to suggest that success comes only when the CEO of the hospital is a physician, it highlights the fact that physician leadership and engagement with respect to clinical programs is important to an organization's success. This stretches far beyond the discussion of hospital leadership and involves the relationships between the hospital and its physician partners. For example, the American College of Cardiology published a white paper in 2009, "Practice Opportunities: Practice Integration, Management Contracts, Hospital Integration," that proposed different practice integration strategies. One strategy outlined was the establishment of valuable partnerships between the cardiac-related practices and the hospital through meaningful service arrangements. In this discussion, it stressed the importance of physician leadership to effectively coordinate across multiple practices and entities so as to focus on the patient and quality of care. The authors listed the following six general prerequisites for a CV practice entering a management agreement with a hospital partner:

- Experience in building, maintaining, and directing a CV program as well as providing leadership among peers and competitors.

- Be successful as a consensus builder, even among competitors.

- Ideally, the hospital administrator and the cardiologist partner will need a legacy of trust or at least the ability to build a trusting relationship about mutual integrity and common goals of improving patient care.

- In general, the cardiology partner will need to be willing to provide education for all of the CV staff members who will participate in the cardiology service line. This would include educating emergency room staff and physicians, CV technical staff, echo lab staff, cardiac cath lab staff, nursing, and so forth, in a continuing attempt to improve quality, meet appropriate quality benchmarks, and establish a more uniform approach to services.

- It is important for the cardiology partner to be malleable and open to change. The management team will often be able to provide both administrative and physician-based information to one another, which may force a "new look" at different ways to deliver ideal care. All of the cardiologists in the practice need to learn and engage as effective partners.

- Though it is not a requirement, it is helpful if the CV specialist or some member of his or her team has a business background. This experience makes it easier to understand contractual issues, capital budgets, and so on.

While clinical faculty/employed physicians and private practices have coexisted for decades in support of successful programs, the increase in the number of employed physicians is adding a new dimension that brings new challenges to the governance, management, and economic models. Both community hospitals and major AMCs are employing physicians for various reasons, including as a defensive measure (i.e., to prevent a competing hospital from doing so). The requirements of a physician leader for a CV service line, center, or institute are also shaped by these dynamics. In open medical staffs at many large health systems, including those that serve as primary teaching hospitals, this is challenging, and it will continue to fundamentally challenge the ability of a CV center or CV institute director to manage and deploy resources effectively. Physicians may be organized in up to three different models: those that remain independent in a practice outside the hospital, employed physicians, and clinical faculty aligned with the medical school (i.e., in a faculty group practice). These challenges further call for a highly integrated, streamlined model (See Figure 5.10) with an empowered physician leader.

FIGURE 5.10

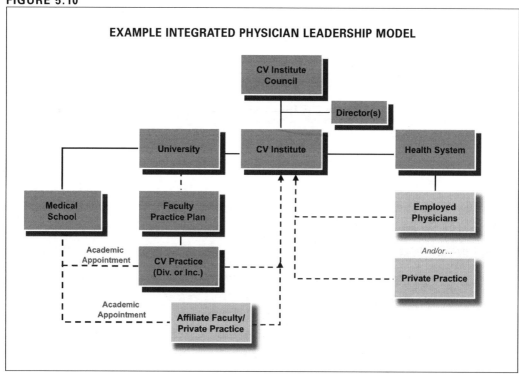

Lessons Learned

- Light coordination across programs to develop a CV service line or center will fall short of delivering patient-centered care through a true multidisciplinary model. A more formally integrated structure, both administratively and financially, will be required.

- Strong and committed physician leadership is a prerequisite to implementing, sustaining, and leading an integrated CV service line or center.

- The size and scale of a hospital and its CV programs may influence the design and degree of integration. Regional health systems and AMCs will experience the most pressure to further integrate CV services across the many subspecialties in coordination with affiliated entities.

- The direction of technology and medicine and continued subspecialization in CV will continue to drive clinical integration, beginning with the medical education and training of tomorrow's CV specialists. This will in turn require more integrated service lines and centers and a more streamlined medical staff leadership model.

- The market can expect to see the emergence of departments of CV medicine beginning in AMCs and large health systems as historical political and financial barriers are removed due to consolidation (e.g., hospital-employed physicians) and the appetite for "full integration" grows.

- Organizations that develop more integrated CV service lines and centers will be better positioned to respond to the new wave of notable market changes, including continued pressure for quality outcomes, payment reform, and hospital-employed specialists.

References

1. Eugene Braunwald, "Departments, Divisions and Centers in the Evolution of Medical Schools," *The American Journal of Medicine,* Vol. 119, No. 6, June 2006, pp. 457–462.

2. Robert M. Califf, M.D., et al., "A Time of Accelerated Change in Academic Cardiovascular Medicine," *Journal of the American College of Cardiology,* Vol. 44, 2004, pp. 1957–1965.

3. Anthony N. DeMaria, M.D., "The Morphing of Cardiovascular Specialists," *Journal of the American College of Cardiology,* Vol. 45, 2005, pp. 960–961.

4. Michael M.E. Johns, "Viewpoint: Developing Integrated Clinical Programs: It's What Academic Health Centers Should Do Better Than Anyone. So Why Don't They?" *Academic Medicine,* Vol. 83, 2008, pp. 59–65.

CHAPTER 6

Developing Employed Cardiovascular Physician Practices

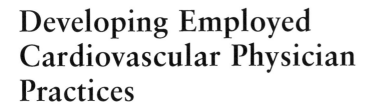

Recent changes to CV reimbursement have fundamentally altered the economics of CV physician practices. These changes have called into question the future viability of the independent practice model for CV physicians. Uncertainty regarding future hospital reimbursement mechanisms and an emerging consensus for the need to prepare for delivering hospital services in a value-based environment are causing hospital and health system leaders to reevaluate care delivery processes for critical service lines, including CV programs. As a result of these and other factors, the number of CV physicians employed by or exploring employment arrangements with hospitals has greatly increased.

Competition among CV programs is intense in most markets across the country. This is due to the magnitude of revenue generated by CV service lines and the significant investment necessary to deliver high-quality CV care. Because the stakes are high, hospital leaders and physicians are often under tremendous pressure to make decisions regarding the employment of CV physicians, many times with incomplete information and in a very short time frame. Once an employment agreement has been implemented, hospital leaders and CV

Strategies for Superior Cardiovascular Service Line Performance © 2010 HCPro, Inc. **133**

physicians frequently discover issues that detract from the efficient delivery of care.

On the other hand, if implemented effectively, the employment of CV physicians can serve as the ultimate physician hospital alignment strategy, generating substantial strategic and financial benefits for the CV service line and the hospital system overall. Successfully executed employment arrangements have the potential to facilitate coordination among CV physicians across multiple subspecialties and better integrate physicians within hospital inpatient and outpatient settings. Employment can also enable CV programs to achieve a competitive advantage by delivering superior quality at lower cost. Successful CV employment arrangements are frequently coordinated with other physician alignment strategies at both the service line and system levels and are designed to anticipate and address a range of issues, from reduced physician productivity to relationship management with independent community CV physicians.

Hospitals should carefully assess these issues when developing a CV physician employment arrangement that can be financially sustainable and enable CV programs to achieve their organizational objectives.

Market Trends Driving CV Physician Employment

Historically, CV physicians have built balanced, independent practices to serve multiple hospitals, often across competing systems. However, recent reductions in reimbursement have fundamentally altered the ability of CV physicians—

     Strategies for Superior Cardiovascular Service Line Performance

primarily within cardiology—to generate acceptable levels of compensation. The deterioration in the economics of the physician private practice model and other factors are compelling hospitals to reevaluate their CV physician alignment strategies, contributing to the growing number of CV physicians and hospitals that are entering into employment discussions.

Physician trends

Intensifying financial, operational, and competitive pressures are major factors driving CV physicians to leave independent practices. These pressures include:

- **Reimbursement:** The overriding factor driving physicians to explore employment options are recent reimbursement reductions. Medicare and many commercial payers have reduced payments in high-volume activities performed in practice settings. Key activities include imaging as well as stress and other ancillary tests. Reimbursement also has been cut for interventional CV services, particularly for outpatient catheterizations and nuclear medicine. These cuts will continue to compress incomes for physicians in independent practices.

- **Increased practice expense:** Compounding revenue issues, CV practice expenses have outpaced reimbursement over the past several years, causing physicians to face greater income pressures. Mandates for electronic medical records (EMR), quality reporting, and coordination of care are creating administrative challenges and costs that many independent practices simply cannot accommodate.

- **Physician recruitment challenges:** Recruitment challenges are increasing as more physicians are becoming disenchanted with the traditional private practice partnership model. Additionally, younger physicians are seeking a work-life balance and are looking for shorter hours, reduced on-call responsibility, and shared or part-time practices.

With the economic viability of the independent practice model in question, physicians are looking to hospitals for the financial stability that employment can provide while seeking an arrangement that will enable them to practice medicine with minimal disruptions from the hospital. Despite the financial stability that employment can offer, most CV physicians are concerned about the potential loss of autonomy and additional administrative burden often associated with this type of arrangement.

Hospital trends

The CV service line typically represents a lion's share of a hospital's contribution margin. Margins generated within the CV service line usually fund less profitable services that are critical for the hospital to accomplish its mission. However, competitive pressures, changes in clinical delivery patterns, and uncertainty regarding future reimbursement sources are compelling hospitals to seek innovative methods of delivering higher-quality CV services at lower cost. The following are critical issues that are causing hospitals to reevaluate care delivery for CV services:

- **Decline in volumes:** Inpatient surgical volumes are declining as CV services continue to transition to outpatient settings. This means hospitals require the services of a robust complement of cardiologists to perform invasive, interventional, and electrophysiology procedures.

 Strategies for Superior Cardiovascular Service Line Performance

Additionally, hospitals must ensure that CV surgeons are available for elective and urgent cases as well as to provide backup coverage for interventional cardiology procedures.

- **Development of integrated care models:** Payment reform, predicated on the notion of bundled payments for specific conditions or episodes of care, and other incentives rewarding prescribed clinical processes and outcomes measures require much stronger alignments between physicians and hospitals. New care models, such as patient-centered medical homes and accountable care organizations, which require hospitals and physicians to accept and share risk, are viewed as methods to promote care coordination, control costs, and improve the quality of patient care.

- **Emphasis on care coordination:** The need to demonstrate clinical quality across the continuum of care requires a stronger affiliation between hospitals and physicians and has spurred a renewed focus on hospitals' key service lines, particularly high-cost, high-volume lines such as CV services.

Physician employment provides hospitals with greater influence over physician resource deployment and incentive design. With these levers, hospitals have the ability to reward behaviors that promote quality and efficiency gains across the entire continuum of care. In the short to intermediate term, employment helps ensure that all necessary specialty skills are in place to maintain a CV service line. In the longer term, employment provides a framework for creating the strongly integrated, data-driven organizational cultures that prepare CV programs for success in the coming era of value-based purchasing.

Common Obstacles to Success

When making decisions regarding physician employment, it is important to apply lessons learned from previous employment cycles. Historical challenges to successful employment arrangements include the following:

- **Diminished physician productivity:** Clinical productivity of employed physicians tends to be lower than their independent colleagues. Productivity declines contribute to inefficient practice performance and result in access issues that impact referring physicians' attitudes and patient satisfaction. Additionally, low productivity affects anticipated downstream volume and revenue and undercuts strategic objectives such as service area or market share growth. To avoid productivity declines, compensation arrangements should encourage physician productivity. Long-term compensation guarantees should be avoided and limited to 12 to 18 months.

- **Physician autonomy:** Often under employment arrangements, practice operations are administered by hospital managers. As a result, physicians are removed from practice operations in hospital-owned environments. This is perceived as infringing on physician autonomy and results in disengagement, which contributes to suboptimal practice performance.

- **Incompatibility between hospital and physician operations:** Hospital and physician services are fundamentally different businesses, and hospital managers may not be experienced in managing physician practice operations. Physician perceptions that hospital-imposed processes

 Strategies for Superior Cardiovascular Service Line Performance

impede care delivery or result in lower productivity levels that ultimately impact compensation are often major sources of friction.

- **Medical staff challenges:** Employment often spurs the perception among independent CV physicians that employed physicians receive favorable treatment by gaining referrals from employed primary care physicians, scheduling block time for procedures performed in the hospital, and so forth. Perceptions of favoritism will alienate independent physicians and could lead to reductions in inpatient admissions and outpatient procedures. Appointment of an employed physician as service line medical director and/or disproportionate representation of employed physicians on service line committees and governance bodies can exacerbate such perceptions.

High-performing hospitals develop structures and systems to anticipate, monitor, and continually address these obstacles. Through governance, management, and operational structures, hospitals create forums for all CV service line physicians to cooperate and maintain appropriate physician autonomy while ensuring that the interests of the hospitals as employers are also protected.

Elements of Successful Employment Models

CV employment models range widely in design, incorporating provisions and structures that reflect the unique business realities of a hospital's particular market. However, the more successful employment models share several commonalities and often incorporate the following six key elements:

1: Application of disciplined decision-making

Too often, hospitals rush the employment decision to meet a perceived crisis. Even in the most urgent circumstances, business discipline and rigor can still be utilized, and timely decisions can be made. Key steps for evaluating employment decisions include the following.

Step 1: Articulate and demonstrate the business need for employment

Hospital and service line leadership must fully understand the magnitude and commitment associated with an employment arrangement. A detailed business assessment should be developed to demonstrate the implications of employing CV physicians, economic and otherwise. An assessment typically includes:

- Conducting a market assessment to determine the economic, operational, and strategic opportunities/challenges associated with a more integrated business model

- Evaluating the full range of economic models to better understand the types of arrangements that are common in the market and to determine the implications of each option

- Developing consensus on the overarching vision and goals for employment

- Conducting a review of the CV practice(s) under consideration to better understand practice performance

- Determining the long-term strategic and financial implications of an employment arrangement, particularly as they relate to the vision and goals

  Strategies for Superior Cardiovascular Service Line Performance

The conclusions and recommendations resulting from the analysis will provide a common understanding of the imperatives for employment.

Step 2: Evaluate medical staff implications of employment

Given the deterioration of the private physician practice model, hospitals are more frequently entering into employment discussions with CV physicians to protect patient volume within the critical CV service line. Hospitals are often faced with three competing strategies:

- A balanced strategy that seeks to protect existing volume and grow incremental market share through limited acquisitions that are pursued only under the most extreme conditions. This strategy is often followed to minimize medical staff tensions and retain favorable relationships with independent CV physicians.

- Targeted acquisition aimed at selectively acquiring physicians who are differentiated based on quality, shared philosophy, and ability to grow incremental market share. Because this strategy requires a greater degree of exclusivity, hospitals risk antagonizing the remaining physicians who do not become employed.

- Broadly utilizing employment as the favored method of developing physician relationships. This is particularly common in markets where it is difficult to recruit or where demand for physician services is still growing. While this allows hospitals to control physician deployment in the market and ensure the availability of physician services, it is an expensive undertaking, requiring significant infrastructure, and can alienate physicians who choose to remain in private practice.

Selecting the appropriate strategy for CV physician employment depends upon a variety of factors, including the distribution of cases among active CV physicians. Circumstances where hospital volume is concentrated with a small number of CV physicians result in a different decision than one where a hospital relies on a large number of CV physicians for case volume. Hospitals must take care to identify the contributions made by various physicians and to quantify the potential consequences of different employment strategies.

A critical resource that is often ignored when hospitals are evaluating employment is the medical staff. When possible, hospitals should solicit input and opinions from existing medical staff members (employed and independent) to confirm assumptions regarding clinical quality and capabilities. These discussions will provide input from prospective referring physicians and generate valuable insights.

Step 3: Determine the appropriate course of action

After evaluating the various alignment options, soliciting medical staff feedback, and evaluating the short- and long-term implications of an employment strategy, hospitals will be better able to make an informed decision on an appropriate course of action.

Step 4: Define the terms of employment

Once employment has been identified as the preferred alignment model, hospitals should work with the CV physician practice(s) to define the specific terms of an arrangement. The employment agreement, which is also a legal contract,

          Strategies for Superior Cardiovascular Service Line Performance

should incorporate provisions to protect the legal and economic interests of both parties. The following factors should be considered:

- **Acquisition structure**: Details regarding how the practice itself will be acquired need to be specifically spelled out in the agreement. Typically, the hospital purchases the practice assets at fair market value rates. In recent years, most transactions have not included large amounts of goodwill. The disposition of the office often depends on whether it is owned by the practice or is located in leased space. Nuclear cameras and other equipment need to be included in the acquisition terms.

- **Compensation methodology**: Because compensation is such a critical element, a component of the agreement should be devoted to describing effective approaches for defining an appropriate compensation methodology. The advantages and disadvantages of common methodologies are also described in a later section of this chapter.

- **Contract term**: Though employment agreements are frequently structured for a term of five years or less, an increasing number of organizations are opting for longer contract terms. Physicians prefer the financial stability associated with a longer contract, and hospitals often consider it part of their broader retention strategy by incorporating vesting provisions into the agreement. For example, some organizations withhold a portion of the physician bonus for a predetermined vesting period; only after completing the predetermined term would physicians be eligible to receive 100 percent of their bonus compensation.

- **Agreement renewal:** Regardless of the contract length, most agreements include a periodic reset every few years to ensure that physician compensation remains commensurate with the market. Organizations utilize a variety of industry benchmarks, preferring those with a wide circulation and large sample size. Due to year-to-year fluctuations within the industry, it is common for organizations to use a three-year rolling industry average to ensure that both the hospital and the physicians are cushioned from random market variations when resetting compensation rates and productivity thresholds.

- **Noncompete agreements:** Noncompete provisions generally restrict physicians from competing within a predefined geographic area for one to two years, or potentially longer if the hospital is acquiring the physician practice. Restrictions range in complexity but generally limit physicians' ability to perform specialty services in competing hospitals/facilities within the employer's primary, secondary, and/or tertiary service areas. In situations where the hospital acquires a physician practice, this noncompete may also include provisions that require physicians to pay back a prorated portion of the practice acquisition costs if they terminate the agreement within a predetermined time frame (e.g., five years from the date of employment). However, hospitals should resist the temptation to overreach in writing a noncompete agreement. In many states, if a judge determines that the time or geographic restrictions are unreasonable to protect the hospital's legitimate economic interests, the entire agreement may be void and unenforceable.

     Strategies for Superior Cardiovascular Service Line Performance

In discussions between hospital and CV physician leadership, it is important to clearly define and agree on the specifics of these employment terms to ensure that both parties have a solid understanding of the key provisions and have truly reached consensus on an arrangement. In particular, a mutually acceptable compensation methodology is one of the most critical factors in a successful employment agreement and should be clearly outlined early in the planning process.

2: Development of optimal employment structure

Creating the optimal vehicle for physician employment and assessing how it may evolve to meet future needs is critical. Hospitals and health systems employ CV physicians in a variety of settings, and each model has its strengths and challenges. Though local conditions may heavily influence which model can or should be pursued in a given market, the most common structures are outlined next.

Multispecialty group

- **Structure:** CV specialties are included in a multispecialty group employed by the hospital.

- **Strengths:** The multispecialty practice model has the potential to deliver high-quality, coordinated care through integrated infrastructure and care systems. High-functioning multispecialty practices are likely to be well positioned for a future reimbursement environment where value is rewarded.

- **Challenges:** In a multispecialty practice environment, there are often tensions regarding the financial trade-offs among the specialties. These tensions are particularly an issue with CV physicians, due to the current reimbursement structure that rewards procedural activity. This type of activity is abundant in CV-related specialties as compared to the cognitive efforts that dominate primary care and other nonprocedural specialties.

- **Solutions:** Compensation structures that acknowledge market differences among specialties while recognizing the contributions, financial and nonfinancial, of all physicians help mitigate inter-specialty friction while promoting integrated care.

CV specialty pods

- **Structure:** CV physicians are organized into single-specialty practices. This is the most common structure for employing CV physicians, especially with the increasing pace of hospitals acquiring existing CV practices.

- **Strengths:** This approach preserves existing CV practice structures, making it easier to implement. Physicians in recently acquired practices prefer this approach because it is the least invasive and minimizes disruptions in practice operations.

- **Challenges:** This model perpetuates practice operational issues and cultures that may be flawed. Once these are established under an employment agreement, it is often difficult to facilitate change. In a pod structure, CV physicians compete with independent physicians for referrals from primary care and other physicians in the community. When referring physicians employed by the hospital refer a higher proportion of patients to employed CV physicians, conflict may ensue. For hospitals that rely upon multiple CV groups, this can be a critical concern.

- **Solutions:** Prospectively establishing guidelines that protect referrals for independent CV physicians and monitoring and reporting referral patterns can mitigate employed/independent conflicts. Involving independent and employed physicians in service line governance may also alleviate potential conflicts.

Heart institute model

- **Structure:** Hospital employs a large number of CV physicians across the continuum of CV subspecialties (noninvasive cardiology, invasive cardiology, interventional cardiology, electrophysiology, cardiothoracic surgery, vascular surgery).

- **Strengths:** In organizations where the heart institute is built on an existing large CV group, financial arrangements and other systems that balance the differences and interests among the subspecialties may already be in place. This model creates a strong, coordinated physician base that can be utilized to serve the strategic needs of the service line.

- **Challenges:** When the institute is built around an existing practice, the group may exercise significant influence in system decision-making. More commonly, the institute combines former competitors into a single group in which rivalries must be addressed.

- **Solutions:** The hospital and physicians must have structures that recognize the strategic partnership while incorporating a system of checks and balances to maintain alignment. In cases where multiple practices have been aggregated, the hospital must proactively work with the CV physicians to develop a leadership structure that is simultaneously flexible enough to preserve practice cultures and avoid perceptions of favoritism but strong enough to drive coordinated effort, efficient deployment of resources, and consistent/effective operations.

An increasing number of hospitals are adopting the heart institute model in response to the growing interest in clinical coordination and value-based care. However, hospitals across the country have successfully incorporated each of these employment structures, tailoring their arrangements to meet the unique needs of their organizations.

3. Establishment of a shared direction

A shared strategic direction is the foundation for successful employed group practices and necessitates hospital and physician consensus on the following aspects:

- **Principles:** Principles represent the values upon which integrated goals and initiatives are built. These principles are meant to be unchanging and will serve as the "sounding board" against which future physician network decisions are made.

- **Vision:** The vision addresses what the employed network wishes to accomplish in the long term.

- **Goals:** Goals are specific results that the integrated group expects to obtain within the first 12 to 18 months of operations.

- **Initiatives:** Initiatives describe how the goals will be realized. They are tactical and encompass both time frames and specific action steps.

4. Clearly defined practice infrastructures

Clearly defined organizational structures are required to create optimal management and governance of any employed physician group. Organizational structures and decision-making constructs also contribute and shape organizational culture. The hospital and CV physicians should jointly develop the group governance, management, and operating structures for the employed group to align with their shared strategic direction for the CV service line.

- **Group governance structure:** Governance defines the structure(s) under which the integrated entity sets its strategic direction, manages fiduciary responsibilities, and oversees organizational performance. Definition of organizational authority and accountability is a critical element in the development of a group's culture. Ultimately, the governing structure must have authority and accountability for ensuring realization of the organizational vision.

- **Management structure:** Management of the group should entail both skilled administrative leaders to ensure efficient operations but should also incorporate physicians to ensure that they are continuing to monitor operations and are invested in the group's success. Specific management structures should aim to appropriately leverage the hospital's employed physician practice capabilities.

- **Operational and clinical integration:** It is also important to define the group's plans to integrate operationally and clinically so the strategic direction can be realized. The areas where decisions will be required in this design phase include definition of the following, among others:

  - Operational and clinical integration structures across network subspecialties

- Program development activities
- Referral and physician recruiting
- Utilization of EMRs
- Performance reporting

5. Determination of the appropriate billing designation

Cuts to office-based CV activities have fundamentally altered the viability of independent cardiology practices; however, payment levels to hospitals for CV activities have remained stable or slightly increased. The incremental costs associated with CV physician employment often cannot be absorbed by hospitals without access to additional revenue streams. Therefore, to offset costs of employment, many hospitals are seeking to convert all or portions of CV physician practices to a provider-based designation.

The Balanced Budget Act of 1997 and subsequent clarifying updates have established specific guidelines on the definition and reimbursement methodology for provider-based clinic designation. Medicare uses the terms "provider-based" and "freestanding" to denote who owns and operates ambulatory clinics.

- Freestanding (also termed physician-based, office-based, non-facility, or place of service [POS] "11") refers to a clinic that is owned and operated by a physician(s)

- Provider-based (also termed hospital-based, facility, or POS 22) refers to a clinic that is owned and operated by the hospital

Under provider-based status, physicians receive a reduced Medicare professional fee for selected services, and nonphysician practice costs are shifted to the hospital. (The reduction in professional fees may not be relevant in cardiology imaging services.) The hospital bills a facility fee to cover the practice costs. This new facility fee typically exceeds the reduction in professional fees and often results in a significant reimbursement advantage, particularly for certain CV imaging services (e.g., nuclear medicine, echocardiography). Figure 6.1 illustrates the differences between reimbursement for freestanding and provider-based clinics.

FIGURE 6.1

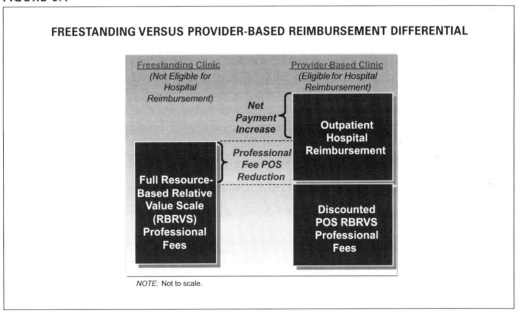

FREESTANDING VERSUS PROVIDER-BASED REIMBURSEMENT DIFFERENTIAL

Freestanding Clinic
(Not Eligible for Hospital Reimbursement)

Provider-Based Clinic
(Eligible for Hospital Reimbursement)

Net Payment Increase

Professional Fee POS Reduction

Full Resource-Based Relative Value Scale (RBRVS) Professional Fees

Outpatient Hospital Reimbursement

Discounted POS RBRVS Professional Fees

NOTE: Not to scale.

The Centers for Medicare & Medicaid Services (CMS) have defined rules regarding provider-based status in nine key areas. Some regulations apply to both on- and off-campus facilities; additional and stricter regulations apply only to off-campus facilities, as shown in Figure 6.2.

FIGURE 6.2

CMS AREAS WITH REGULATIONS FOR PROVIDER-BASED STATUS

On Campus	Off Campus
• Licensure	• Ownership and control
• Clinical integration	• Joint ventures
• Financial integration	• Management contracts
• Public awareness	• Administration and supervision
• Location/proximity to main provider	

Consequently, provider-based designation has significant operational and organizational implications relating to key functional processes and systems, such as physician and hospital billing, information system interactions, and staffing mix. Patients also may be financially impacted through their copayment amounts.

Regardless, there is typically a significant reimbursement advantage to converting CV practices to provider-based billing status. However, the conversion requires thoughtful planning and preparation to ensure compliance with regulation, assessment of competitive risk, evaluation of the impact on patients, and implications on physician activity within the clinic. Experts should be utilized to evaluate the potential overall impact and to develop strategies to mitigate risk exposure for each of these considerations.

6. Alignment of physician compensation with organizational priorities

Developing a physician compensation methodology that aligns physician incentives with hospital CV programmatic priorities is critical to ensuring that organizational objectives are achieved. Effective compensation methodologies incorporate variables that encourage clinical productivity, quality and coordination of care, financial stability, and other variables identified by hospital leadership.

Compensation for physicians in CV-related specialties is somewhat more complex and nuanced than in other specialties that are typically employed by hospitals. Cardiology practices often include physicians with subspecialty capabilities. If a hospital is seeking to emphasize and facilitate development of CV subspecialists, compensation arrangements must incorporate incentives to allow subspecialization to occur. These mechanisms may be different than in a general cardiology practice. For example, special provisions for subspecialties that expand service line market share but may not generate commensurate practice revenues, such as pediatric cardiology, may be considered. Similarly, compensation formulas should include consideration for nontraditional activities that support service line goals, such as participation in community outreach and screening events.

In addition, there are likely to be differences, sometimes significant, in compensation amounts and incentives in CV physician practices acquired by hospitals. Real and perceived inequities will exacerbate conflicts in an already volatile environment. Hospitals that are employing CV physicians from multiple groups should develop strategies to, over time, transition to a common compensation formula with consistent incentives. In addition, thoughtful consideration and planning should be given in order to transition from legacy compensation arrangements to a revised methodology.

Compensation goals and objectives

The critical first step in designing a physician compensation plan is to articulate goals and objectives. These goals should tie to corresponding CV service line and broader organizational objectives. Ultimately, compensation goals established at the outset of a planning process are the criteria against which alternative compensation arrangements can be evaluated. Common goals include the following:

- Philosophical objectives
  - Alignment of compensation with productivity
  - Transparency
  - Administrative simplicity

- Clinical objectives
  - Improved patient/physician experience and access to care
  - Enhanced subspecialization
  - Clinical integration

- Programmatic objectives
  - Reduced costs
  - Program development
  - Market share growth and outreach

Figure 6.3 outlines common physician compensation arrangements; each model has its advantages and disadvantages. In practice, characteristics from these various models are often combined to create incentives to reward desired behaviors and activities.

 Strategies for Superior Cardiovascular Service Line Performance

FIGURE 6.3

COMPENSATION MODELS

Model 1: Income Guarantee

Structure	A guaranteed salary regardless of practice productivity or finances, set at a predetermined compensation target. Typically based on an industry-wide percentile and periodically adjusted to reflect changes in productivity.
Advantages	Stabilizes income, clinical model, and culture for physicians; easy for hospitals to administer.
Disadvantages	Offers little incentive for increased production and the fewest opportunities to align physician and hospital incentives. May result in diminished productivity.
Mitigating Considerations	Minimum work thresholds mitigate productivity risk but can be difficult to negotiate.
Risk/Potential	Low risk/low upside potential.

Model 2: Base Salary Plus Production Bonus

Structure	A guaranteed salary supplemented by a bonus based on work relative value units (RVUs) or total RVUs beyond a set threshold. The bonus may be based on individual productivity, total group productivity, or a combination of both.
Advantages	Potentially increases physician income; aligns financial incentives with hospital.
Disadvantages	Offers less income stability for physicians and no incentive for nonclinical physician activities, such as administrative contributions to the CV service line.
Mitigating Considerations	Could incorporate additional incentives for nonclinical work.
Risk/Potential	Moderate risk/moderate upside potential.

FIGURE 6.3

COMPENSATION MODELS (CONT.)

Model 3: Base Salary Plus Multiple Bonus	
Structure	A guaranteed salary supplemented by bonuses based on factors such as productivity, quality and outcomes, outreach and referral relationships, program development, and patient satisfaction.
Advantages	Flexibly aligns incentives for nonclinical activities. Aspects such as standardizing clinical practices may be self-funding.
Disadvantages	Developing service line metrics and valuing nonclinical work can be difficult. May weaken the direct link between compensation and production.
Mitigating Considerations	Time studies could be utilized to set payments. RVUs or other productivity metrics could also be included in the formula.
Risk/Potential	Moderate risk/moderate to high upside potential.
Model 4: Pure Productivity	
Structure	No salary guarantee. Physicians are compensated at a fixed rate per work RVU or total RVU, either individually or as a group. The compensation rate may increase for production above certain thresholds.
Advantages	Potentially increases physician income. Ensures hospital costs are in line with productivity.
Disadvantages	Offers limited income stability for physicians and does not align incentives for physician participation in nonclinical service line work.
Mitigating Considerations	Could incorporate additional incentives for nonclinical work.
Risk/Potential	Moderate risk/moderate to high upside potential.

        Strategies for Superior Cardiovascular Service Line Performance

FIGURE 6.3

COMPENSATION MODELS (CONT.)

Model 5: Group Collections Less Expenses	
Structure	Physicians are paid based on net collections less allowances for fixed and variable practice costs, including office space, billing and IT services, malpractice insurance, medical supplies, and clinical assistants.
Advantages	Maintains physician autonomy and clinical and shared compensation models. Rewards cost containment. Ensures hospital costs are in line with productivity.
Disadvantages	Physicians are not protected from future pay cuts and have little opportunity to align hospital and physician incentives for nonclinical service line work.
Mitigating Considerations	Despite the preservation of autonomy, physicians are generally not inclined to adopt this model, as it does little to address physician risk.
Risk/Potential	High risk/moderate to low upside potential.

Compensation model trends

While a variety of compensation structures are possible, certain general conditions influence what terms are practical to include, and as market conditions evolve, so will compensation structures.

In the current environment, productivity is king. Hospitals, in general, recognize that production-driven plans will need to evolve to reflect changing practice patterns and economics, but there is a reluctance to get too far ahead of reimbursement changes.

Production-based compensation plans (typically measured in work RVUs) continue to be the favored methodology for hospitals, and they often utilize productivity tiers that disproportionately reward high producers and provide strong incentives at the margin. These plans reflect the current economics of physician payment, which is still based almost entirely on clinical work measures.

While hospitals are increasingly incorporating small incentives for citizenship and service line performance into their compensation models, these measures are a relatively new trend. Defining, valuing, tracking, and assessing outcomes for these measures can prove difficult. They can provide a huge boon to executing service line strategies, though, and more institutions are starting to incorporate these incentives and making them a larger portion of total compensation.

Emerging patterns: Coordination, quality, and efficiency will rule

In CV-related specialties, organizations are recognizing issues created by the distortions inherent within the RVU system that result in misaligned work RVU values relative to physician effort. Innovative mechanisms have been implemented to reduce internal competition among physicians, foster subspecialty integration, and improve overall group cohesion.

- Use of service incentives in physician compensation models is an emerging trend that will continue to grow, particularly in light of ongoing healthcare reform efforts that emphasize patient outcomes and episode-based care.

 Strategies for Superior Cardiovascular Service Line Performance

- The primary compensation methodology will likely evolve into episode-based service incentives. To encourage the coordination of services that will be required to profit under this model, physician compensation will increasingly be based on a variety of performance objectives, including outcomes, patient satisfaction, and cost control.

Financial Implications of CV Physician Employment

To succeed, CV employment arrangements must be financially viable. Because the financial impact of CV physician employment is system-wide and endures over years, it should be considered in terms broader than the profitability of the practice itself.

General trends

- Hospitals may experience initial and ongoing losses from CV physician employment due to practice acquisition costs, needed infrastructure support (e.g., EMR transitions), shifts in referral patterns, and issues with physician productivity.

- Profitability of an employment model often relies on hospitals' ability to ensure continued physician productivity and involvement in service line planning/development.

- Through proper development of an employment arrangement, organizations can achieve service line profitability despite the initial costs and risks of CV practice acquisition.

Profitability drivers

Employing CV physicians will drive system profitability in a variety of ways:

- **Hospital revenue:** CV physicians generate substantial direct and down-stream (e.g., CV surgery) revenue through inpatient admissions, procedures, and outpatient services. Employing independent medical groups often results in the transition of a substantial percentage of their remaining revenue, resulting in large incremental revenue gains for the hospital.

- **Physicians' professional revenues:** Under an employment arrangement, physicians' professional revenues will transfer to the hospital in addition to the income generated from their incremental hospital volumes. Properly structuring an employment arrangement with shared financial incentives will help ensure that physicians continue to increase their clinical productivity, improve their practice performance, and potentially capitalize on increased economies of scale.

- **Ancillary revenue:** Many CV practices generate a significant portion of their revenue in an office/lab setting, and much of this revenue is related to the physicians' ancillary services (e.g., cardiac catheterizations, echocardiography, nuclear medicine). Often these ancillary volumes could be billed as provider-based, potentially resulting in sharp reimbursement gains from Medicare and select commercial payers. However, gains on these services may not be enough to completely offset the cost of employing physicians.

 Strategies for Superior Cardiovascular Service Line Performance

- **Recruitment platform:** Developing an employment model that will help build a strong recruitment/retention platform will allow hospitals to save on the long-term costs associated with securing/maintaining their CV physician base.

Due to these incremental revenue streams, the enterprise-wide contribution margin generated by CV physician employment typically exceeds the initial transaction costs of CV practice acquisition, along with any ongoing practice operating losses; however, the program's financial success will also be contingent on the development of a financially sustainable employment arrangement, particularly as it relates to the physicians' compensation methodology.

Financial success indicators

Employment arrangements are more likely to be financially sustainable if they are properly structured to include the following key factors:

- **Shared financial incentives:** Hospitals are increasingly developing compensation models that utilize shared financial incentives to achieve predefined service line performance measures (e.g., cost savings, device standardization).

- **Physician leadership and service line involvement:** To encourage productivity and profitability, hospitals are providing physicians with an active role in CV service line management as well as direct accountability for reaching practice goals.

- **Performance monitoring**: To monitor the performance of employed physician practices, service lines often implement a dashboard of key metrics (e.g., inpatient/outpatient volumes, readmission rates, Physician Quality Reporting Initiative measures). Both industry and internal benchmarks are typically used to diagnose and track physician performance.

- **Budgetary trigger**: Ultimately, unforeseen business realities may come into play that will affect the year-to-year cash flows of the CV service line. Structuring an employment arrangement that includes a budgetary trigger helps mitigate the risk of large financial losses. Some compensation agreements incorporate a budgetary trigger that limits the amount of money available for a physician's bonus if the CV service line is operating at a loss. This type of provision ensures that the hospital and the CV physicians will share the risk associated with the CV service line's annual performance.

Lessons Learned

Properly structured, the employment of CV physicians can be beneficial to both parties, and the most successful employment models typically result from the following six-step approach:

1. Utilize a rigorous and disciplined evaluation process when assessing employment decisions

2. Develop an appropriate employment vehicle to meet current and future needs

   Strategies for Superior Cardiovascular Service Line Performance

3. Proactively establish a shared vision and set of goals that define success for the employment arrangement

4. Incorporate group structures where possible

5. Develop an appropriate billing designation to maximize reimbursement opportunities

6. Create incentives within the compensation plan to align physicians with the hospital's organizational priorities

Attaining Programmatic Recognition

Recognition in the form of awards and accreditations is usually the outcome of developing a strong CV program and delivering high-quality patient care. It is important for your hospital to be recognized because it enhances the marketability of the program and provides additional substance in promotion, as well as providing differentiation in the market and creating added focus around key areas of the service line. In the case of health plan recognition, it can also mean active channeling by the health plan to your center, which can result in obvious volume and market share gains. Competition for CV patients, which typically garner high margins, has increased significantly over the past 15 years. This has led to hospitals looking for ways to differentiate their CV service lines to gain a distinct advantage over their competition.

There are a significant number of CV care recognition programs available for hospitals, but what they measure and what they reward varies widely. Hospitals can receive accolades for robust programmatic development, for achieving superior quality outcomes, for having the best reputation, or by implementing processes that enhance care delivery. Measurements for these designations are uniquely designed by each organization. When managers and physicians are developing objectives for pursuing an award or ranking, it is important to understand the methodology and criteria for achievement. Program recognition can be a boon to a CV service line in terms of creating greater emphasis on quality or solidifying the program's reputation. However, given the number of different options available, it is important that leadership set its sights on award programs that align with the service line's strategic goals. It is also vital to analyze whether the designation is achievable based on the resources available. This chapter examines how leaders can determine which designation to pursue and provides specific information on some of the most prominent awards.

Designation Selection

Pursuing and successfully achieving a prominent program designation requires a strong organizational commitment in terms of time and resources. Therefore, the decision of which designations to pursue should be a strategic one. Achieving the recognition desired requires an organized initiative, which is shaped by the specific recognition program targeted. When evaluating the potential recognitions to be targeted, the leadership team should answer the following questions:

- What specifically do you hope to achieve by receiving the recognition?
  - Market share gains
  - Enhanced quality
  - Improved coordination of care
  - Improved operational efficiency

- Enhanced recognition for specific cardiac services

- Accreditation of clinical programs

- Stronger overall reputation in the market

- Does the recognition leverage the service line's current strengths?

- Is the focus of the recognition in keeping with the service line's strategic focus?

- How well is the award or designation recognized in the market by patients? By physicians?

- Does the program meet the requirements of the designation in terms of issues such as volume thresholds or program scope?

- What is the difference between the program's current performance along key metrics compared to levels that will need to be achieved to receive the award?

- What is the likelihood of being able to achieve the designation?

- What will be the administrative requirements to achieve the award?

- How will physicians need to be involved to achieve the award? Are the necessary relationships currently in place?

- How much time and resources will be needed to launch the initiative?

These questions highlight the need to create a deliberate and methodical process for targeting the initiatives to be pursued. By going through this process, the hospital will also begin to formulate a work plan for launching the required work steps. The outcome of this process should be an organizational commitment to which designations will be pursued and a high-level plan for deployment of the resources needed to achieve it.

Overview of Rankings and Accreditation for Cardiac Programs

Not surprisingly, a number of organizations offer awards and accreditations for CV programs, and the metrics and the methodologies used vary greatly. Cardiac program recognitions range from accreditation for specific imaging modalities to designations from health insurance companies. Payers, private organizations, associations, and media publications all offer awards and recognitions (see Figure 7.1 for an overview).

While there is a wide range of awards and accreditations available, the following are some of the most widely recognized designations nationally:

- **Thomson Reuters** – 100 Top Hospitals®: Cardiovascular Benchmarks

- **HealthGrades** – Specialty Excellence Awards™

- **U.S. News & World Report** – Best Heart & Heart Surgery Hospitals

- **Society of Chest Pain Centers (SCPC)** – Chest Pain Center Accreditation and Heart Failure Accreditation

These awards are highlighted not only because they are well recognized within the CV services arena, but also because they are available nationally and their focus represents a broad programmatic outlook. The metrics and methodology used by each of these organizations in awarding designations are examined in detail next.

FIGURE 7.1

SAMPLE OF CV SERVICES DESIGNATIONS

Organization	Designation
American Association of CV and Pulmonary Rehabilitation	• Rehabilitation Program Certification
Intersocietal Accreditation Commission	• Vascular Laboratory Accreditation • Echocardiography Accreditation • Nuclear Medicine Laboratory Accreditation
American Heart Association, Inc. (AHA) – Mission: Lifeline	• Recognition for Non-Percutaneous Coronary Intervention (PCI) ST-Elevation Myocardial Infarction (STEMI) Referral Centers
	• Recognition for PCI/STEMI Receiving Centers
AHA – Get With The Guidelines	• Coronary Artery Diseases Performance Achievement Award • Heart Failure Performance Achievement Award
Blue Cross and Blue Shield Association	• Blue Distinction Centers for Cardiac Care
CIGNA	• Center of Excellence for Cardiac Catheterization • Center of Excellence for Coronary Artery Bypass Grafting • Center of Excellence for Heart Attack • Center of Excellence for Heart Failure • Center of Excellence for Heart Valve Replacement
UnitedHealth	• Premium Designation Program – Cardiac Care • Premium Designation Program – Cardiac Surgery • Premium Designation Program – Cardiac Rhythm Management
Aetna	• Institutes of Quality Cardiac Care Facilities

Please note: This is a representative list, and there are a number of other programs that offer well-recognized designations on both a local and national basis.

Methodologies

It is important to understand the methodologies because the focus of each is different, and the metrics utilized vary as well. The methodologies used should be a key factor in deciding which designation is the optimal one to pursue. As will be detailed, some awards focus on quality metrics, others look at process improvement, and still others include a reputational component. The program that would be able to achieve one award may not be successful when attempting another because of differences in program focus and strengths and weaknesses within the service line. Therefore, it is important to know how success is determined in order to understand which recognitions are attainable and are in keeping with the service line's strategy.

Thomson Reuters

The Thomson Reuters 100 Top Hospitals®: Cardiovascular Benchmarks study is based on a series of metrics that measure the quality and cost of cardiac care provided.[1] To be included in the study, hospitals must have open-heart surgery capabilities and meet specific volume thresholds. Winners are categorized in one of the following three categories: teaching hospitals with CV residency programs; teaching hospitals without CV residency programs; and community hospitals.

In 2009, Thomson Reuters selected nine categories—eight performance measures and one procedure volume threshold—for use in reviewing hospitals to produce benchmarks for superior performance (see Figure 7.2). The categories are equally weighted (the weights for the two risk-adjusted complications add

Strategies for Superior Cardiovascular Service Line Performance

FIGURE 7.2

CALCULATION AND WEIGHTS OF THOMSON REUTERS PERFORMANCE METRICS

Category	Calculation	Weight
Risk-Adjusted Medical Mortality Index (Acute Myocardial Infarction [AMI] and Heart Failure)	Number of actual deaths divided by number of expected deaths.	AMI = 0.5
Heart Failure = 0.5		
Risk-Adjusted Surgical Mortality Index (Coronary Artery Bypass Graft [CABG] and PCI)	Number of actual deaths divided by number of expected deaths.	CABG = 0.5 PCI = 0.5
Risk-Adjusted Complication: Postoperative Hemorrhage Index	Number of CABG and PCI cases that developed hemorrhage or hematoma divided by number of expected cases.	0.5
Risk-Adjusted Complication: Postoperative Infection Index	Number of CABG and PCI cases that developed postoperative infection divided by number of expected cases.	0.5
Core Measures Score	Mean of all heart failure core measures and AMI core measures.	AMI = 0.5 Heart Failure = 0.5
Percentage of CABG Patients With Internal Mammary Artery Use	Number of CABG surgeries using internal mammary arteries divided by total number of CABG surgeries.	1.0
Procedure Volume Threshold	Number of PCI procedures meets the minimum threshold of 149, and number of CABG surgeries meets the minimum threshold of 35.	CABG = 0.5 PCI = 0.5

FIGURE 7.2

CALCULATION AND WEIGHTS OF THOMSON REUTERS PERFORMANCE METRICS (CONT.)

Category	Calculation	Weight
Severity-Adjusted Average Length of Stay	Length of stay for AMI, heart failure, PCI, and CABG, considered separately, is adjusted based on severity of illness using refined diagnosis-related groups (RDRGs) and compared to the appropriate comparison group.	1.0
Severity- and Wage-Adjusted Cost Per Case	Costs for AMI, heart failure, PCI, and CABG, considered separately, are adjusted based on severity of illness using RDRGs and differences in local wages, using the Centers for Medicare & Medicaid Services (CMS) wage scale adjustment. Costs are then evaluated against the appropriate comparison group.	1.0

1. Expected data is determined by grouping patients with similar characteristics (age, sex, ICD-9-CM diagnosis, and comorbidities) to produce expected, or normative, comparisons. Thomson Reuters developed a normative database consisting of approximately 20 million annual discharges. A standard logistic regression model is used to estimate the risk of mortality or complications for each patient diagnosis.

2. All AMI core measures were used except for Heart Attack Patients Given Fibrinolytic Medication Within 30 Minutes of Arrival, because only a limited number of hospitals reported this measure.

to 1.0). Within each of the hospital comparison groups, hospitals were ranked based on their total weighted score, and the hospitals with the best scores were selected as the 100 Top Hospitals benchmarks.

Data for its 2009 study primarily came from two publicly available data sets: Medicare Provider Analysis and Review (MEDPAR) and the Medicare Cost Report. In addition, Thomson Reuters looked at the U.S. Department of Health & Human Services (HHS) Hospital Compare core measures. It is important to note that Thomson Reuters uses two years of data for most of its measures, and the most up-to-date data lags a year behind the study (e.g., the 2010 benchmark study is based on 2008 and 2009 data). Therefore, significant improvements in performance measures may not be acknowledged by the study for two years.

HealthGrades

HealthGrades Specialty Excellence Awards™ is one of the most well-known consumer resources for the public's use in evaluating healthcare providers.[2] Through its Specialty Excellence Awards, HealthGrades recognizes hospitals performing in the top 10 percent in each of 15 specialty care areas.

There are five CV-related Specialty Excellence Awards:

- Cardiac Care Excellence Award

- Cardiac Surgery Excellence Award

- Coronary Intervention Excellence Award

- Vascular Surgery Excellence Award

- Heart Transplant Excellence Award

The first four CV excellence awards are based on mortality ratings. The Heart Transplant Excellence Award is based on three-year survival rates and wait-list mortality rates. HealthGrades utilizes two data sources for determining its Specialty Excellence Awards in CV services: historical Medicare inpatient data from the MEDPAR database and the registry of transplant recipients. The Specialty Excellence Award designation is determined by employing compilations of hospital ratings that HealthGrades provides for a set of related procedures or diagnoses. The hospital must have experienced 30 cases across three years, or at least 5 cases in the most current year, to be ranked. (Sample sizes can be quite small, making the accuracy of rankings for qualified hospitals with small programs questionable. Transplant awards do not have minimum thresholds.)

Five stars are assigned when the actual performance was better than expected and the difference was statistically significant. Three stars are assigned when the actual performance was not significantly different from the expected performance. A single star is provided when the actual performance was worse than expected and the difference was statistically significant.

The methodologies for choosing the Specialty Excellence Award winners are determined by evenly weighting the star rating for each of the procedures or diagnoses measured. Some of the awards require hospitals to have minimum

     Strategies for Superior Cardiovascular Service Line Performance

service offerings. The top 10% of hospitals within each specialty area are selected as HealthGrades Specialty Excellence Award recipients (unless otherwise noted by HealthGrades). Figure 7.3 shows the components of the CV Specialty Excellence Awards and their required minimum service offerings.

FIGURE 7.3

COMPONENTS OF THE CV SPECIALTY AWARDS

Award	Procedure or Diagnosis Category	Minimum Service Offerings
Cardiac Care Excellence Award	• Coronary bypass surgery • Valve replacement surgery • Coronary interventional procedures (PTCA/angioplasty, stent, atherectomy) • Heart attack • Heart failure	• Hospital must provide coronary bypass surgery • Hospital must receive a rating in three of the other four categories
Cardiac Surgery Excellence Award	• Coronary bypass surgery • Valve replacement surgery	• Hospital must receive a rating for one of the two categories
Coronary Intervention Excellence Award	• Coronary interventional procedures (PTCA/angioplasty, stent, atherectomy)	
Vascular Surgery Excellence Award	• Resection/replacement of abdominal aorta • Carotid surgery • Peripheral vascular bypass	• Hospital must receive a rating in all three categories
Heart Transplant Excellence Award	• Three-year patient survival rating in heart transplantation • Wait-list mortality rating in heart transplantation	

U.S. News & World Report

With a circulation of nearly 1.3 million and a popular Web site, the Best Hospitals ranking is well known among educated consumers of healthcare. Because *U.S. News & World Report*'s[3] program focuses on treating high-acuity tertiary and quaternary diseases, it has become the most prominent ranking for academic medical centers. In contrast to the Thomson Reuters study, outcomes are only one of the three categories that make up the scoring system for *U.S. News & World Report*'s Best Heart & Heart Surgery Hospitals rankings. The other two categories are structure and process. These three categories were weighted evenly until the 2009 study, when a patient safety index component was added. The patient safety index is worth 5% of the overall score and is distributed evenly to the outcomes and process categories. As of 2009, outcomes and process have higher weights at 35%, whereas structure is weighted at 30%.

A hospital must meet multiple criteria to be eligible for the ranking. First, an eligible hospital must satisfy at least one requirement around bed size, academic affiliation, or equipment availability. In the second stage, hospitals need to pass a minimum threshold for number of discharges and offer certain cardiac services. The 2009 rankings required a hospital to have a minimum of 980 cardiac discharges, with at least 500 of them being surgical. (The discharge volume thresholds are reviewed annually and are subject to change.) The hospital must also offer cardiac intensive care, adult interventional cardiac catheterization, and adult cardiac surgery to be considered. In 2009, only 767 hospitals were eligible for the Heart & Heart Surgery ranking after the second stage.

   Strategies for Superior Cardiovascular Service Line Performance

Outcomes

The outcomes category uses 30-day risk-adjusted mortality to measure quality of care. The same actual-divided-by-expected equation conducted in Thomson Reuters' 100 Top Hospitals and HealthGrades' Specialty Excellence Awards is used to calculate hospital scores, but limits its analysis to high-acuity and challenging procedures. The source for this data is also MEDPAR, and three years of data are utilized, with adjustments made for low-volume hospitals.

Structure

The structural dimension is defined as "the tools, human and otherwise, available at hospitals for treating patients." The structure category for Heart & Heart Surgery consists of a number of indexes, including:

- Key technologies
- Volume
- Nurse staffing
- Trauma center
- Patient service
- Intensivist
- Nurse Magnet hospital

The majority of the information used to develop the structure score is from the latest American Hospital Association Annual Survey Database.

Process

Evaluation in this category is based on physician specialists providing national hospital rankings for their specialty areas. For Heart & Heart Surgery, 200 board-certified cardiologists, electrophysiologists, and thoracic surgeons from the four census regions of the country (50 physicians in each region) were mailed surveys. Respondents were asked to list as many as five hospitals nationally that provide the best care for serious conditions in the specialty. The responses were weighted to adjust the response rate so as to normalize nominations across the four regions. Responses from the most recent three-year surveys were utilized to arrive at the results.

Patient safety index

In 2009, *U.S. News & World Report* introduced a patient safety index, a new index score that attempts to measure patient safety in hospitals. This index is calculated from a subset of the Agency for Healthcare Research and Quality's Patient Safety Indicators (PSIs) as well as two additional indicators (death in low-mortality DRGs and failure to rescue). The PSIs potentially show adverse outcomes that are associated with below-standard healthcare. The PSIs are adjusted for population variation as well as case mix so that hospitals can be appropriately compared. Hospitals are then scored based on their percentile rankings.

SCPC

Unlike the awards and acknowledgments discussed previously, The Society of Chest Pain Centers[4] promotes protocol-based medicine and process improvement, as opposed to outcomes measurement. The pursuit of accreditation from

SCPC requires that a hospital reflect on its current processes for care delivery and discover where improvement can occur. Accreditation is available to hospitals with cardiac programs, no matter the scope or scale of services offered. Currently SCPC offers two accreditations:

- Chest Pain Center Accreditation

- Heart Failure Accreditation

To begin the process, the hospital purchases a manual that directs it through the accreditation process. The hospital performs a gap analysis to see where its processes and methodologies are lacking in comparison to an accredited facility. The hospital then forms multidisciplinary care teams to develop and implement strategies to improve processes. Once implementation has occurred, the hospital applies for accreditation. Once the application is submitted, SCPC assigns a review team. SCPC reviews the submitted documentation and then conducts a site visit at the hospital.

There are eight key elements in which an organization must demonstrate expertise:

- Emergency department integration with the emergency medical system

- Emergency assessment of patients with symptoms of possible acute coronary syndrome (ACS), and timely diagnosis and treatment of ACS

- Assessment of patients with low risk for ACS and no assignable cause for their symptoms

- Process improvement

- Personnel, competencies, and training

- Organizational structure and commitment

- Functional facility design

- Community outreach

The reviewers develop a report of their findings and submit it to the Accreditation Review Committee. The committee will then decide whether the hospital deserves accreditation. To achieve accreditation, facilities must have successfully met or exceeded the criteria during the on-site review. The review process is collaborative and provides feedback, education, and resources to assist the facility in addressing gaps and improving processes.

Lessons Learned From Award-Winning Heart Programs

To better understand what distinguishes award-winning hospitals from others, heart program leaders from a number of the country's award-winning cardiac programs were interviewed. Interviewees represented both community hospitals and AMCs from across the country whose programs had been honored with some of the awards and recognitions previously described. The following represent key themes voiced by interviewees regarding what helped their organizations achieve excellence in CV services.

Pursuit of program recognition

Hospitals employ a variety of tactics when considering how actively to pursue programmatic recognition. Some top-performing programs create initiatives to actively pursue an award, whereas others simply focus on exceeding industry quality benchmarks. In the latter case, while there is not a focus on targeting specific awards, the programs benefit from looking at some of the same key metrics utilized in the awards. Many programs participate in private registries and databases, such as those offered by the American College of Cardiology, The Society of Thoracic Surgeons, University HealthSystem Consortium, and the American College of Surgeons. The hospital is able to achieve the quality awards because the data they are measuring and comparing overlaps with the measurement being conducted for Thomson Reuters 100 Top Hospitals or HealthGrades Specialty Excellence Awards.

Interviewees representing hospitals ranked by *U.S. News & World Report* voiced that they do try to actively improve their rankings. This is more difficult than simply focusing on improving quality measures because of the many diverse components that make up scoring for the *U.S. News & World Report* Best Hospitals rankings. Enhancing standing in these rankings requires not only that a hospital improve its cardiac program, but also that a set of physicians in the industry recognize this. A hospital can make significant strides in enhancing its heart program, but if the physicians who participate in the ranking process are unaware of the improvements, the hospital will experience limited movement in the survey because of the subjective nature of the reputation-based process score. It is paramount for a hospital to enhance its national reputation in the minds of peer organizations and physicians to improve its ranking. It is also imperative that physicians from these ranked organizations be seen by their counterparts as experts in their fields. A hospital's medical staff giving speeches and presentations at national forums, as well as publishing research in scientific journals, is vital to developing the national reputation of the organization.

Interviewees also noted that hospitals looking to improve their *U.S. News & World Report* rankings also should carefully examine where there are gaps in their structure scores. Investment in structure components, such as developing a Level II trauma center or a transplant program or becoming a Nurse Magnet hospital, is a significant time and resource commitment. Investment in these components has a much greater impact than investment in just cardiac services and must be evaluated to ensure it is in accordance with the entire organization's strategic vision.

Key features of award-winning organizations
Documentation
All of the hospitals interviewed have a strong commitment to accurate documentation, and there is an understanding that correctly documenting acuity is vital to an organization's standings in its outcomes-based rankings. As was detailed previously, components of Thomson Reuters 100 Top Hospitals, HealthGrades Specialty Excellence Awards, and *U.S. News & World Report* Best Hospitals outcomes measures were based on dividing actual measures by expected measures. When acuity levels are not accurately documented, which typically results in a lower acuity, the expected outcomes value (the denominator in the equation) is higher than what it should be, thus artificially lowering the outcomes scores. It is possible that a high-quality hospital is not in

consideration for acknowledgment because of inaccurate documentation. Therefore, it becomes important to focus on accurate documentation not only for billing and coding reasons, but also to ensure that the program is being compared appropriately.

Create a culture focused on excellence

Three points continued to be reiterated by interviewees from high-achieving organizations. First, they have created a culture that strives for excellence. Second, they take time away from the daily provision of care and bring teams together to determine how to improve. Third, they measure and track every initiative. Award-winning hospitals have developed expectations for quality and achievement. While many organizations aim to be above the median, many of the organizations interviewed aimed for the 90th percentile or above for all measures. These organizations are also "pushing the envelope" with their quality measures. A number of the hospitals interviewed have developed their own unique measures for services such as electrophysiology, for which few measures currently exist with professional organizations. Their reason for doing this is simple: it is difficult to improve what you cannot measure.

As was voiced by those interviewed, the tool sets used by award-winning hospitals for process improvement and quality enhancement can be quite different, but these functions have become part of the fabric of each hospital's culture. Some hospitals require that management learn Six Sigma or Lean techniques to mitigate variation or streamline processes. One of the hospitals interviewed has developed a research institute, funded by grants, that focuses on quality improvement, whereas another hospital has a quality academy where physicians and staff can learn how to conduct quality and process improvement projects. A common characteristic of these hospitals is that they have all created a culture of improvement and accountability. They use techniques to standardize care and remove human error. Examples include ensuring that all providers use evidence-based protocols to deliver care, utilizing checklists to ensure accuracy, and providing standard follow-up care to discharged patients. These standards are reviewed and updated to make sure they reflect the latest in evidence-based research. Each of these hospitals has high expectations for performance, and simply maintaining the status quo is unacceptable.

A culture has also been created in regard to data transparency and dissemination of data to all parties that can affect the process. High-achieving hospitals have come to realize that decisions must be made based on data, especially in attempts to change physician behavior. One organization interviewed developed a balanced scorecard that evaluates quality data at the physician level and disseminates the unblinded data to all physicians in that specialty. The logic for sharing such revealing data is twofold. First, it brings a degree of productive competition to improvements in quality and efficiency. Second, it is apparent that as data reporting continues to become more sophisticated, this information will eventually be publicly available.

Physician integration

Another commonality found between the hospitals interviewed was physician integration. While the degree of integration varied, all of the hospitals made physicians an integral part of their quality improvement projects. There is a common understanding among these accomplished organizations that physicians are the drivers of care, and without their support of and buy-in to quality improvement, only limited results can be achieved.

The majority of the recognized hospitals interviewed had employed CV physicians. A number of them also had dyad leadership models in place, incorporating the physicians into service line management. The hospitals with employed medical staffs believed that their high level of integration gave them a distinct advantage in their ability to engage physicians in quality improvement initiatives.

Results of Achieving Program Recognition

In a healthcare market increasingly characterized by consumerism, achieving programmatic recognition can aid in changing patient care-seeking behavior. Although physician referrals and word-of-mouth still are primary drivers of patient choice, many patients are conducting research on potential programs before going to the hospital for CV care. Attaining programmatic recognition can both enhance the reputation of the program and also force the service line to become more rigorous in its focus on key quality metrics and the way data is reported. Making the attainment of programmatic awards a key strategy raises the prominence of the initiatives, thereby making them a focal point. In a largely undifferentiated market, having one or more prominent awards can be a way to create a recognizable brand in the eyes of patients and even referring physicians. A top ranking can also help create a destination service for the cardiac program, changing patient migration patterns and enhancing volumes. However, in highly competitive markets that have multiple hospitals with strong cardiac brand recognition, the impact of attaining one of these awards may be muted.

These accolades help hospitals in other ways as well. They give staff members a sense of pride because their efforts have been recognized. They help with the recruitment of physicians and staff who want to be associated with a program that is seen as providing excellent care. Other service lines view similar achievements as more attainable, and the awards create a more tangible understanding of the road map for success. Finally, receiving a service-specific award can create a halo effect for the hospital.

References

1. For more information, please see *www.100tophospitals.com/top-cardio-hospitals*.

2. For more information, please see *www.healthgrades.com/hospital-solutions/ratings-and-awards*.

3. Conducted by the research firm RTI International. For more information, please see *http://health.usnews.com/best-hospitals/rankings/heart-and-heart-surgery*.

4. For more information, please see *www.scpcp.org*

Navigating the Challenges of
Cardiac Reimbursement

The CV service line is a major revenue generator for hospitals, but it has been challenged by the constant need to respond to technological advancements that have driven up costs for implantable devices and have led to volume shifts to the outpatient setting. Both commercial and government payers have taken aim to control the costs of CV procedures and associated diagnostic services through payment bundling and other aggressive reimbursement and contracting initiatives. The Centers for Medicare & Medicaid Services payments to cardiologists and hospitals alike have taken sustained and significant hits and are still at significant risk. It is paramount that the CV service line receives favorable reimbursement from its portfolio of third-party payers, particularly given the preponderance of CV patients who are over the age of 65, as Medicare reimbursement is not typically sufficient to maintain financial stability.

Understanding the Current Reimbursement Landscape

Medicare reimbursement and trends

Even though Medicare dictates the reimbursement terms only for the services provided to its beneficiaries, the impact of its reimbursement methodologies and priorities extend into the commercial insurance realm as well. Most commercial payer contracts are based, in part, on Medicare payment methodologies or are linked to Medicare payment levels. Thus, trends in Medicare reimbursement impact reimbursement from nearly all payers. Given the importance of understanding Medicare reimbursement, the following sections provide an overview of the key trends that have taken place and are continuing to evolve in both the hospital and physician-office setting for CV services.

Hospital Inpatient Reimbursement

CMS' philosophy has been to fine-tune its Medicare inpatient payment methodologies in an effort to control costs, compensate hospitals based on the severity of illness of their patients, and introduce incentives for improving the quality of care. This philosophy is apparent when one reviews changes that have been implemented in recent years—and the trends suggest what form future changes will take.

DRG to MS-DRG

One of the largest changes related to inpatient hospital reimbursement occurred on October 1, 2007, when CMS transitioned from a Diagnosis-Related Group (DRG) methodology to one based on Medicare Severity DRGs (MS-DRGs). The replacement of the prior DRG classification system with the MS-DRG system represented a major step toward increasing the degree with which payments to hospitals are aligned with the intensity of resource use. The concept of collapsing paired DRGs into base MS-DRGs and then subdividing the base DRGs into additional DRGs with varying weights based on

Strategies for Superior Cardiovascular Service Line Performance

complications and comorbidities was devised to correlate payments with intensity of resource use. The new weights are assigned to account for the most severely ill patients with major complications or comorbidities (MCC), those with complications or comorbidities (CC) who are less severely ill, and the least ill without CC/MCC. In addition to subdividing the DRGs into MS-DRGs, CMS also revised its methodology for calculating the relative weights from charge-based to cost-based and modified its approach to how outlier cases and transfers are handled.

The payment weights for MS-DRGs with MCCs increased significantly, while those for less severe cases either decreased or only slightly increased. Therefore, the impact of the transition to any given hospital has been based upon its ratio of severely ill patients compared to those who are less sick, as well as the hospital's ability to appropriately code to support the presence of a CC or MCC. Hospitals that treat sicker patients and can code accordingly have seen reimbursement increases, whereas those that treat less acute patients have seen reimbursement declines due to the changes.

While the impact on any one hospital has depended upon its patient mix, the transition to MS-DRGs and the other changes initially had a negative effect on cardiology revenues as a whole. For example, an American Hospital Directory study of the impact of the 2008 Inpatient Prospective Payment System (IPPS) found that the transition to MS-DRGs resulted in an estimated 5.2% decrease in reimbursement for CV surgery (equivalent to a shift of $621 million to other medical services).[1] On the other hand, studies by RAND

Health demonstrate that the MS-DRG methodology was successful at redistributing payments to more closely reflect the severity of illness than the previous CMS DRG-based model.[2] The results of these studies are indicative of the complexity of generalizing national changes and thus highlight the importance of analyzing changes at the specific hospital level.

Subsequent updates to the IPPS demonstrate that Medicare is continuing its efforts to more closely align payments to the actual resources used. CMS is also making changes that hold facilities more accountable for the cost and quality of the services that they provide. A guiding principle in subsequent changes to Medicare IPPS and resource-based relative value scale (RBRVS) payment methodologies is to increase value to Medicare beneficiaries by improving the correlation between the amount of payment and the cost of providing services.[3] Ongoing policy changes are in reaction to the Medicare Payment Advisory Commission's (MedPAC) 2005 recommendations that DRGs be refined to more fully capture differences in severity of illness and that DRG relative weights be based on cost rather than charges, be dependent on the national average of hospitals' relative values in each DRG, and be adjusted to account for differences in the prevalence of high-cost outlier cases in each DRG.[4] Most recently, these principles have been manifested through the implementation of various quality measures, the way hospital-acquired conditions (HAC) impact reimbursement, implementation of new revenue codes in response to "charge compression," reimbursement for replacement implantable devices, and further updates of select DRGs.[5] A good example of how MS-DRGs continue to be modified to reflect resources used in different procedures is the recent subdivision of MS-DRG 245 into MS-DRGs 245

 Strategies for Superior Cardiovascular Service Line Performance

(AICD Generator Procedures) and 265 (AICD Lead Procedures). This change makes the assigned payment more appropriate for these distinctly different procedures.[6]

Charge compression

St Jude Medical defines charge compression as *"...the practice of applying a higher percentage markup to lower cost items and services and a lower percentage markup to higher cost items and services reported in the same cost center, leading to understatement of the true cost of cases using more expensive items."*

This issue has been addressed by making adjustments to the Medicare cost reports. For example, charge compression historically was an issue for high-cost cardiac implantable devices, such as pacemakers or defibrillators. In order to more accurately reflect the costs of these devices, Medicare has updated the cost reporting process by adding a new cost center for implantable devices.[7] Because there is a three-year lag between cost report submission and the availability of data, the impact will not be apparent until at least 2012.

Implantable devices

To further align reimbursement with hospitals' actual costs for implantable devices, Medicare also reduced payments for implantable devices replaced under warranty or other circumstances under which the hospital receives a credit from the manufacturer of at least 50% of the cost of the device.[8] While addressing implants to align payments with prices, proposed 2011 reimbursement for the DRGs in which medical devices are commonly used continue to reflect annual increases of 2% to 4%.[9] This has allayed some industry concerns that CMS would continue to put pressure on the cost of cardiology medical devices, as it did following the initial implementation of MS-DRGs.

Value-based purchasing

In addition to responding to cost differences, CMS continues to refine its value-based purchasing initiative, which was implemented in response to the Deficit Reduction Act of 2005. The implemented policies include reducing payments when certain HAC occur during a Medicare beneficiary's hospital stay.[10] Of the 12 HAC that preclude higher CC or MCC MS-DRG reimbursement, the specific conditions most pertinent to cardiac services include surgical-site infection, mediastinitis following coronary artery bypass graft, and vascular catheter-associated infection. Of course, most of the other nine measures could also be related to any hospital admission, including those for cardiac care.

The other major component of CMS' value-based purchasing initiative is quality. CMS continues to update the Reporting Hospital Quality Data for Annual Payment Update program.[11] Under the proposed 2011 program, hospitals will be eligible to receive a full market-basket increase (2.4% for 2011) if they participate by submitting data. Participation includes reporting on 27 chart-abstracted measures, including several that are cardiac-related. There are also 15 claims-based measures, such as mortality and readmissions for heart attack and heart failure. Finally, there is a structural measure for participation in a cardiac surgery registry on all 46 measures. The FY 2011 program retains measures related to treatment for heart failure and heart attack, which rank among the 10 most common Medicare inpatient diagnoses and are two of the highest contributors to Medicare costs.[12]

Future trends

As healthcare reform occurs, the full impact of future updates to IPPS on reimbursement for cardiac services cannot be predicted with certainty. The recent trends suggest that there will be continuing focus on reimbursement paralleling cost and the use of various programs to require quality improvement and accountability for the value of services provided to Medicare beneficiaries. Innovative and creative methods that are currently being tested in various pilot projects are discussed later in this chapter.

Hospital Outpatient Reimbursement

Over the past two decades, there has been a national trend of treatment moving from the inpatient to the outpatient setting, and CV services have been no exception. During this period, cardiology groups across the country moved to take advantage of favorable reimbursement from Medicare for diagnostic testing, imaging, and selected interventional procedures in an office-based setting. As a result, volume and revenue migrated away from the hospital and into physician practices. CV procedures are often performed on an outpatient basis, and many are available in physician offices depending on Certificate of Need regulations, including the following:

- Echocardiogram

- Stress echocardiogram

- Transesophageal echocardiogram (TEE)

- Electrocardiogram (EKG)

- Stress test

- Holter monitoring

- Noninvasive arterial Doppler studies

- Cardiac catheterization

- Cardiac electrophysiology

- Cardiac nuclear imaging/positron emission tomography

- Cardiac diagnostic imaging (CT, MRI)

In addition to a shift in the care delivery setting, the volume of these tests/procedures performed also increased. For example, one study by a radiology trade publication estimated that volume of imaging at nonhospital settings grew 13% more quickly than hospital-based volumes between 2003 and 2006.[13] The financial impact on Medicare of these increased volumes has resulted in a reconsideration of reimbursement levels. Beginning in 2006, CMS implemented significant changes in the Medicare Physician Fee Schedule (MPFS) that reduced reimbursement for cardiac-related services in non-facility-based settings (physician offices). These changes reduced the practice expense component assigned to nonhospital-based outpatient procedures, such as cath lab procedures.[14]

Conversely, since 2006, hospital reimbursement for these services, when provided in a facility setting, has slightly increased. The reimbursement under the Ambulatory Payment Classification (APC) system for the same cath lab procedures increased by 5% in 2007 and 8.5% in 2008.[15] The following section discusses these changes, which are expected to continue to impact cardiac services over the coming years.

Inpatient versus outpatient reimbursement levels

CMS has increased overall hospital reimbursement for cardiology outpatient procedures performed in facility-based settings, yielding a nearly 6% increase per APC on average between 2008 and 2010. In addition, during that same time period, there was an expansion of codes available for reimbursement, including pulmonary and intensive cardiac rehabilitation, allowing a greater array of services to be reimbursed. Notably, CMS moved forward with these changes despite the fact that many industry organizations that side with physicians expressed significant concern over the reimbursement trend. Increasing reimbursement for these procedures in the hospital setting appears to show a clear emphasis by CMS on centralizing where these procedures are taking place and shifting volume back to a facility-based setting. As an example, based on the changes implemented by CMS, office-based reimbursement to physicians for an echocardiogram (CPT 93306) has dropped nearly 42% from 2006 to 2010. Conversely, Outpatient Prospective Payment System (OPPS) or facility-based reimbursement for the same procedure increased by approximately 19% during that time period. (National professional reimbursement under MPFS for an echocardiogram (CPT 93306 in 2010) in an office setting was $416.88 in 2006 and $242.62 in 2010. Medicare hospital OPPS reimbursement for an echocardiogram in a hospital outpatient setting was $378.76 in 2006 and $450.97 in 2010.)[16]

Not coincidentally, the resulting trend that began in 2008 has been the sale of facilities, such as cardiac catheterization labs, by physicians to hospitals. The resulting loss in reimbursement has also driven many cardiologists to seek employment arrangements with hospitals to support historical compensation levels.

Direct supervision

In 2010, CMS clarified "direct supervision" requirements for outpatient services to mean that the physician or nonphysician practitioner must be present anywhere on the hospital campus and immediately available to furnish assistance and direction throughout the performance of the procedure. Previously, supervising personnel were required to be physically present to earn credit for supervision. The supervision requirements will now also allow certain nonphysician practitioners—specifically physician assistants, nurse practitioners, clinical nurse specialists, certified nurse-midwives, and licensed clinical social workers—to provide "direct supervision" for all hospital outpatient therapeutic services that they are authorized to personally perform according to their state scope of practice and hospital privileges. The combination of these two changes will allow a greater range of services to be offered at less expense for hospitals because professional personnel can supervise more than one service at a time.

However, for services furnished in an off-campus provider-based department, "direct supervision" will continue to mean that the physician or nonphysician practitioner must be present in the off-campus provider-based department and immediately available to furnish assistance and direction throughout the performance of the procedure. This policy further supports the trend toward shifting the care setting to the hospital.

ASC reimbursement

CMS is continuing to refine reimbursement for cardiac procedures performed in an ambulatory surgery center (ASC) setting, as it is set to complete the transition to the broader set of procedures allowable at ASCs in 2011. The most recent changes applied a 1.2% increase to the conversion factor for calendar

Strategies for Superior Cardiovascular Service Line Performance

year 2010. CMS also updated the list of device-intensive procedures and covered ancillary services and their rates to be consistent with the OPPS update. Many cardiac procedures have yet to be added to the ASC allowable list, but it is expected that the list will continue to grow as these procedures are shown to be safe in an ASC setting.

Future trends

The desire by Medicare to develop bundled payments will almost certainly encompass cardiac outpatient services. The combination of multiple services in a single APC—for instance, APC 8000 Cardiac Electrophysiological Evaluation and Ablation—will continue in the future. From cardiac stress tests and annual echocardiograms being bundled with preventive care for seniors to cardiac rehabilitation therapy for patients who suffer heart attacks, cardiology is expected to be included in the wave of bundled payments.

Physician Services

At the core of Medicare physician reimbursement is the MPFS, which is calculated based on the RBRVS that was first introduced in 1992. The MPFS defines the payment levels for the majority of the professional services provided by physicians (in all settings of care) and of their employed clinical staff (in a physician office). (Payment levels for office-administered drugs, lab services, and supplies are defined based on different fee schedules.)

A large proportion of Medicare revenue to the typical cardiology practice has historically been derived from diagnostic imaging, testing, and select invasive cardiology services. The graphics in Figure 8.1 depict the typical percentage of Medicare revenue derived from each type of service performed by cardiologists

FIGURE 8.1

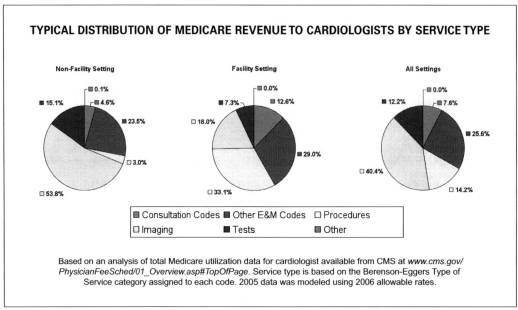

TYPICAL DISTRIBUTION OF MEDICARE REVENUE TO CARDIOLOGISTS BY SERVICE TYPE

Non-Facility Setting

0.1%
4.6%
15.1%
23.5%
3.0%
53.8%

Facility Setting

0.0%
12.6%
7.3%
18.0%
29.0%
33.1%

All Settings

0.0%
7.6%
12.2%
25.6%
40.4%
14.2%

■ Consultation Codes ■ Other E&M Codes □ Procedures
□ Imaging ■ Tests ■ Other

Based on an analysis of total Medicare utilization data for cardiologist available from CMS at *www.cms.gov/ PhysicianFeeSched/01_Overview.asp#TopOfPage*. Service type is based on the Berenson-Eggers Type of Service category assigned to each code. 2005 data was modeled using 2006 allowable rates.

in a facility (hospital) and non-facility setting (physician office). Changes implemented by Medicare have reduced the payment levels for services central to the economics of cardiology practices.

Reimbursement changes impacting cardiology

Medicare continues to implement changes in the methodology underlying the MPFS that have had a significant impact on the reimbursement for cardiology services, depending on the setting in which they are provided. In 2009, CMS instituted the bundling of Doppler echocardiogram codes under the single CPT code 93306. In 2010, payment for consultations were eliminated, the four-year transition to a new practice expense relative value unit (RVU) methodology was initiated, and payments for SPECT Myocardial Perfusion Imaging (SPECT

Strategies for Superior Cardiovascular Service Line Performance

MPI) were bundled under code 78452. CMS will transition to the changes that result from new practice expense RVU methodology over a four-year period: 25% in 2010; 50% in 2011; 75% in 2012; and 100% in 2013.

These and other changes have combined to create a trend of declining reimbursement for the services that represent the most significant revenue sources for the typical cardiology practice. The graphic in Figure 8.2 shows historic reimbursement trends for key procedures/services billed to Medicare by cardiologists. Based on all physician services billed to Medicare, reimbursement for the services presented in the graphic represent over 45% of total Medicare

FIGURE 8.2

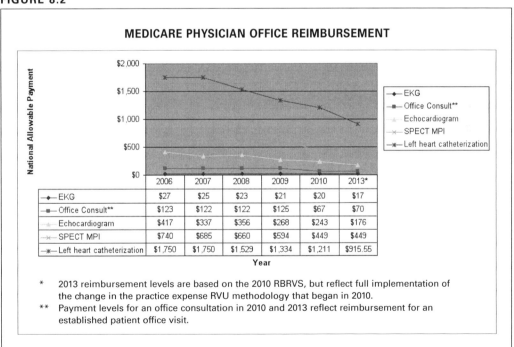

MEDICARE PHYSICIAN OFFICE REIMBURSEMENT

	2006	2007	2008	2009	2010	2013*
EKG	$27	$25	$23	$21	$20	$17
Office Consult**	$123	$122	$122	$125	$67	$70
Echocardiogram	$417	$337	$356	$268	$243	$176
SPECT MPI	$740	$685	$660	$594	$449	$449
Left heart catheterization	$1,750	$1,750	$1,529	$1,334	$1,211	$915.55

Year

* 2013 reimbursement levels are based on the 2010 RBRVS, but reflect full implementation of the change in the practice expense RVU methodology that began in 2010.

** Payment levels for an office consultation in 2010 and 2013 reflect reimbursement for an established patient office visit.

payments to cardiologists. (Based on an analysis of Medicare utilization data.)[17] As this demonstrates, Medicare reimbursement has fallen dramatically, and no significant increases are forecasted for the next few years.

Incentives for setting of care

For cardiology practices, as with others specialties, the total (physician and hospital) Medicare reimbursement in a provider-based setting has historically been higher than in a physician-office-based setting. Depending on the service mix and proportion of Medicare patients, the total reimbursement for services provided in a hospital outpatient (provider-based) clinic can be significantly higher than in an office-based setting, as shown in Figure 8.3. This difference is due to the payment of a separate facility fee to the hospital, based on APC rates, in addition to a site-of-service (SOS) reduced physician payment in a provider-based setting. When the reduced professional fee under the provider-based designation is combined with the facility fee, total payments typically exceed those in an office-based clinic.

FIGURE 8.3

MEDICARE PHYSICIAN FACILITY REIMBURSEMENT

2009 Code/ Description	APC	2009 Medicare Reimbursement						2010 CPT Code	APC	2010 Medicare Reimbursement						Changed in Provider-Based Opportunity 2009 to 2010	
		Office-Based	Provider-Based			2009 Provider-Based Difference				Office-Based	Provider-Based			2010 Provider-Based Difference			
		Physician	Physician	Hospital	Total	Dollars	Percent			Physician	Physician	Hospital	Total	Dollars	Percent	Dollars	Percent
99213 Office Visit	0605	$61.31	$44.72	$68.96	$113.68	$52.37	85.4%	99213	0605	$66.74	$49.41	$69.68	$119.09	$52.35	78.4%	-$0.02	0.0%
93000 EKG	0099	$20.92	$9.02	$26.09	$35.11	$14.19	67.8%	93000	0099	$20.28	$9.22	$26.56	$35.78	$15.50	76.4%	$1.31	9.2%
99243 Office Consult	0605	$124.79	$97.38	$68.96	$166.34	$41.55	33.3%	99213	0605	$66.74	$49.41	$69.68	$119.09	$52.35	78.4%	$10.80	26.0%
93306 Echocardiogram	0269	267.61	71.77	$431.37	$503.14	$235.53	88.0%	93306	0269	242.62	17.16	450.97	$468.13	$225.51	92.9%	-$10.02	-4.3%
SPECT Myocardial Perfusion Imaging																	
78465		$485.10	$78.99	$774.13	$853.12												
78480		$49.77	$17.67	Bundled	$17.67												
78478		$59.51	$32.10	Bundled	$32.10												
Total	0377	$594.38	$128.76	$774.13	$902.89	$308.51	51.9%	78452	0377	$449.48	$80.38	$775.09	$855.47	$405.99	90.3%	$97.48	31.6%

 Strategies for Superior Cardiovascular Service Line Performance

While the reimbursement levels for physician services have declined and will likely continue to move in this direction, the reimbursement levels for facility reimbursement to hospitals for services provided in a hospital outpatient clinic (facility setting) have remained materially unchanged. These factors have combined to increase the magnitude of the difference in total reimbursement in a provider-based setting. Collectively, these changes have created an economic incentive for cardiology practices to pursue more financially integrated relationships with hospitals (see Figure 8.4) and to consider the transition of office-based practices to provider-based status.

FIGURE 8.4

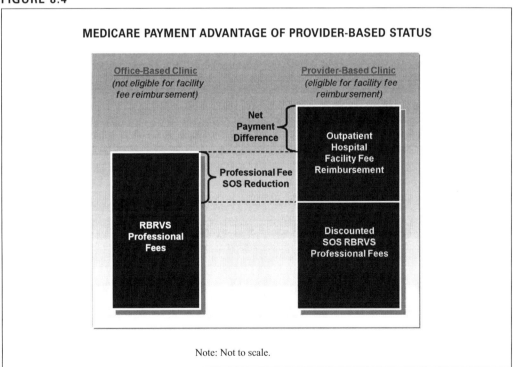

MEDICARE PAYMENT ADVANTAGE OF PROVIDER-BASED STATUS

Office-Based Clinic
(not eligible for facility fee reimbursement)

Provider-Based Clinic
(eligible for facility fee reimbursement)

Net Payment Difference

Outpatient Hospital Facility Fee Reimbursement

Professional Fee SOS Reduction

RBRVS Professional Fees

Discounted SOS RBRVS Professional Fees

Note: Not to scale.

Commercial Reimbursement and Trends

Many of the trends and changes discussed previously also apply to commercial plans, given that their rates and methodologies are tied to Medicare. On the other hand, not all changes implemented by Medicare are implemented by commercial payers. Therefore, it is important to carefully read and interpret contracts to understand if and how changes in Medicare will impact reimbursement from third-party plans. It is also important for hospitals and physicians to negotiation protections in contracts that prohibit commercial plans from unilaterally following Medicare methodologies that may have negative financial consequences.

The following subsections explore some of the reimbursement trends that are likely to impact commercial plans for both hospitals and physicians.

Hospital services

Move to case rates

Many commercial payers are moving to case-rate-based methodologies and away from per diem or percentage of charge methodologies. The move to case rates can be both financially and operationally beneficial to the hospital, particularly since hospital case managers and other clinical staff are already accustomed to managing the patient stay for Medicare patients. The case-rate-based methodology can help to focus efforts on managing the care and ensuring the appropriate length of stay. In addition, health plans will almost always lift stringent medical and utilization management requirements that may have previously placed administrative burdens on hospital case managers.

It is important, however, that hospitals negotiate appropriate stop-loss and high-cost implantable device protection when moving to a case-rate-based methodology. Many commercial health plans have initiatives in place to bundle implant costs into the case rate and to limit stop-loss protection. If these protections are not put into place or are not set appropriately, major negative financial consequences to the hospital are possible.

Use of variations on standard DRG methodology

For a variety of reasons, commercial payers continue to evaluate and implement DRG systems that are different than the CMS MS-DRG. For example, the All Patient Refined-DRG system is being implemented because it allows for even more cost variation and is more representative of non-Medicare populations. The use of any DRG system by commercial payers may also involve the implementation of their own weighting methodologies. It is important to understand any payer-specific adjudication rules that may impact their proprietary DRGs.

Transparency in pricing

While not yet widespread, it is certain that efforts to control costs, improve service or quality, and make the cost of care more transparent to patients will impact reimbursement for cardiology services. One example that bears watching is that of states trying to regulate prices in an attempt to slow down the rate of premium increases. For example, Massachusetts is reportedly considering a bill to limit physician and hospital reimbursement to within some defined multiple of Medicare rates. Cost controls such as these will make it even more difficult for providers to cover their costs.

Value-based pricing and pay for performance

As healthcare reform occurs, it is anticipated that managed care organizations will focus on developing collaborative approaches with providers that focus on rewarding improvements in outcomes or cost savings.

Physician services

Commercial insurers reimburse physicians based on a variety of methodologies, which may include standard fixed fee schedules by the current procedural terminology (CPT) code or negotiated conversion factors multiplied either by the standard fixed fee schedules or by Medicare RBRVS schedules.

Standard fixed fee schedules

Health plans are increasingly requiring that physicians be paid based on the plans' standard fee schedules or some negotiated multiple of the schedules. These schedules have mirrored Medicare for cardiac services in an attempt to control costs, particularly for diagnostic services and procedures provided in the physician-office setting.

Conversion factors

Conversion factors are also negotiated in certain markets and are applied to either payer-specific standard fixed fee schedules or the Medicare RBRVS.

The most common application of conversion factors is coupled with Medicare RBRVS. Payers may utilize a single conversion factor that applies to all provider services or vary the conversion factor by service type to reflect payer priorities and/or market dynamics.

          Strategies for Superior Cardiovascular Service Line Performance

Adding to the complexity, contracts are not necessarily based on the current year's RBRVS. Moreover, some commercial payers vary in how frequently they update the applicable RBRVS year. Whereas some payers lag by several years, others update the RBRVS on an annual basis. Therefore, when calculating the estimated reimbursement or negotiating an agreement, it is critical to define the specific Medicare RBRVS year (and quarter, because Medicare RBRVS is updated on a quarterly basis by CMS) to which the conversion factor is applied.

Keys to Effective Commercial Contract Negotiations

As hospitals and physicians continue to experience cuts in Medicare reimbursement year after year, they have increasingly begun to depend on commercial revenue to offset those losses. That being said, it is important to maximize health plan contract performance through negotiation of optimal rates and language provisions that affect financial performance. The following subsections address selected key components of any successful contract negotiation process.

Employ a data-driven approach

Solid data and a well-reasoned approach are keys to negotiating better reimbursement rates. Most of the data needed to initiate the process should be readily available for hospitals and medical groups from their automated billing systems. The assessment of contract performance for medical groups should be based on the CPT codes that account for at least 75% of the total practice charges. Hospitals can most effectively evaluate contract performance by comparing the amount paid under the particular commercial payment methodology with what would have been paid using Medicare rules. The assessment also should compare the agreement in question with the other major payers that make up the bulk of commercial reimbursement. To provide an apples-to-apples comparison, the allowed contracted rate for each payer should be calculated as a weighted average percentage of Medicare and as compared to fully allocated costs. This exercise will also serve other objectives, such as providing medical groups/hospitals with the ability to understand and/or model the following:

- For medical groups, the mix of services and settings of care for the practice that drive total payments under a given contract:
  - Office or facility SOS
  - ASCs
  - Drug administration
  - Labs, supplies, and durable medical equipment

- For hospitals, how the mix of services and other variables impact the overall reimbursement:
  - Inpatient and outpatient services
  - Outlier or stop-loss provisions
  - Carve-outs for high-cost implants or specific cases
  - Lesser of cost or charges

- The impact of RVU changes based on the mix of services for medical groups

- The effects of changes in payment methodologies for hospitals

- The impact of changes in contract terms during negotiations, including:
  - Conversion factors
  - Change in payment methodologies
  - SOS adjustments

Payers are resistant to granting sweeping fee increases. However, with the proper data in hand, a stronger case can be built for negotiating increases for individual services that can have major favorable financial consequences.

Understand contract language nuances

In the ever-changing healthcare climate, favorable contract provisions can help providers maintain revenue stability. Significant changes in Medicare policies and payment terms related to professional and facility reimbursement for echocardiograms, nuclear stress tests, consult codes, inpatient and outpatient surgical procedures, and others have unfavorably shaken up cardiology practices and impacted hospitals. A high level of anxiety persists among hospital and practice administrators and physicians regarding the influence that these changes will have on commercial insurers. However, certain provisions can be negotiated to protect against significant, unanticipated material changes in payment provisions. Specifically, language should be incorporated into agreements that provides for budget-neutral adjustments when changes in Medicare payment policies cause an unfavorable financial impact on reimbursement during the term of the agreement.

Strategies for providers seeking to protect commercial revenue streams include:

- Defining the process and timing for calculation, communication, and implementation of rate and methodology changes, including:
  - DRG weighting methodologies and changes
  - Codes defined in RBRVS (typically annual)
  - Drug code updates (typically quarterly)
  - Payment bundling rules

- Defining the methodology for reimbursement of codes that are not currently defined in the MPFS, including:

  - New codes added since the last fee schedule update
  - Drugs codes newly approved by the FDA
  - Codes not otherwise classified or specified (NOC/NOS codes)

- Addressing elements of the hospital agreements, including:

  - How DRG or outpatient case weights are adjusted
  - The impact of annual charge description master increases on charge-based reimbursement
  - Inpatient and outpatient payment bundling rules and changes
  - Inflation
  - Stop-loss or outlier provisions for case rates or per diems
  - Payment for high-cost implantables and drugs

With the appropriate provisions in place, providers can gain additional assurance that the agreement they are entering into will perform as anticipated.

Other key contracting provisions should be closely examined before finalizing an agreement, as they can have significant influence on contract operations and performance. See Figure 8.5.

Providers should consider all opportunities to improve their negotiating leverage by utilizing key data to support their position, emphasizing network presence, and highlighting key accomplishments and community involvement.

FIGURE 8.5

KEY CONTRACT PROVISIONS

Contract Provision	Key Provision Detail
Claims Submission and Payment	A reasonable time frame for claims submission and payment obligations should be established.
Key Definitions	Particular attention should be paid to definitions for clean claims, medical necessity, payer entity, and covered services.
Incorporation of Other Documents	Any material provisions should be included in the contract and not just incorporated by reference.
Termination	The provider should have the right to terminate without cause.
Access to Data	Access to data should be reciprocal for both parties.
Unilateral Changes	The insurer should not be able to unilaterally change the terms of the agreement without consent of the provider or prior notice of change to the provider via certified mail.
Retrospective Denial	The plan should not be able to retrospectively deny payment for services already authorized through pre-authorization or concurrent reviews. At the very least, there must be a reasonable time limit for any retrospective changes.
Audit and Reconciliation	The scope of audit rights should be defined, and time limits specified.
Appeals	Agreements should have a fair and objective appeals process to appeal denials and other adverse payment decisions.
Dispute Resolution	Dispute resolution options include informal mediation, nonbinding/binding mediation, and nonbinding/binding arbitration. Providers should seek advice from counsel and consider the ramifications of giving up the right for litigation.

Providers are facing an ever-growing pressure to contain overall costs, such as labor, malpractice, and supplies. They are also being held accountable for the quality of care and outcomes, as well as the overall cost of medical care to the health plans. With the trends toward healthcare reform, providers should be proactive in working with commercial health plans to achieve fair reimbursement for their current efforts, as well as to design innovative approaches that will also benefit the patients and insurers.

Innovative Measures of Performance/Payment Methodologies

Both government and commercial payers are piloting innovative payment methodologies around cardiac services, with the focus on driving both improved outcomes and cost savings. The value-based payment methodologies under study by government and commercial payers can be categorized into four major models. A summary of each model and the advantages and disadvantages of each can be found in Figure 8.6.

P4P

Pay for Performance is intended to promote an adherence to evidence-based care and eliminate the incentives for providers to perform unnecessary services. Measures vary from program to program, but most use a combination of measures that include:

- Clinical quality and effectiveness

- Utilization and cost management

- Patient satisfaction

FIGURE 8.6

VALUE-BASED PAYMENT METHODOLOGIES

Model	Advantages	Disadvantages
P4P	• Simplicity and clarity • Focused approach produces results on select measures	• Only limited dollars are tied to outcomes • Focused approach limits comprehensive overhaul • Has not typically facilitated hospital/physician alignment
Bundled Payments	• Facilitates hospital/physician alignment • Comprehensive, outcomes-based approach	• Complexity • Organizational structure requirements between physicians and hospitals limit participation
Patient-Centered Medical Home (PCMH)/Guided Care Models	• Involves focused management of patient populations • Enhances patient satisfaction • Has shown positive results for both medical expense savings and improved clinical outcomes • Can be implemented in conjunction with other payment reform efforts	• Requires major infrastructure investments • Necessitates cross-practice coordination and cultural transformation • Complicates physician compensation in the multispecialty group setting • May negatively affect hospital reimbursement under current payment structures
Accountable Care Organizations (ACO)	• Facilitates hospital/physician alignment • Aligns financial incentives • Major financial opportunity • New risk models have the potential for greater focus on clinical outcomes	• Complexity • Infrastructure requirements are significant • Care management sophistication, and focus limits participation and success • Past risk models have historically lacked clinical outcomes basis • Major financial risk

- Administrative involvement

- Patient safety

The Medicare Hospital Value-Based Purchasing (VBP) program would provide value-based incentive payments to acute care IPPS hospitals that meet certain quality standards, beginning in 2012. In 2013, hospital payments would be adjusted based on performance under the VBP program. Hospitals that meet or exceed performance would receive incentive payments. Funding for the payments would come from a reduction in reimbursement to all hospitals, with the reduced payment being redistributed in the form of an incentive payment in the same year. Hospital performance would be publicly reported, and there would be a mechanism for appeal.

Bundled payments

Bundled payments are payments that encompass more than discrete patient encounters, including global and packaged payments. Medicare is currently studying numerous payment reform pilots specific to cardiac services. Medicare's acute care episode (ACE) demonstration is encouraging collaboration and quality by using bundled payments. The goal of this demonstration is to use bundled payment to better align incentives for both hospitals and physicians, leading to better quality and greater efficiency in the care that is delivered. ACE is a three-year project with bundled payments for specific CV and orthopedic services. Twenty-eight cardiac and nine orthopedic inpatient surgical services and procedures were chosen because of their high volume, high cost, and available quality metrics. Under the program, a single payment is made for Part A and Part B Medicare services provided during an inpatient stay. Eligible organizations are defined as entities with at least one physician group and one hospital that routinely provide the procedures included in the demonstration. Sites have the option to reward individual clinicians, teams of clinicians, or other hospital staff members who succeed with measurable clinical quality and efficiency improvements.

Medicare is also considering other bundled payment pilots and has stated that if they are successful in reducing costs and increasing quality, the Secretary of the U.S. Department of Health & Human Services (HHS) would be required to submit an implementation plan in FY 2016, for incorporation of new Medicare payment models beginning in FY 2018.

PCMH/guided care models

PCMH is a model of care in which each patient has an ongoing relationship with a personal physician who leads a team that takes collective responsibility for patient care. While the primary care physician typically (but not always) assumes the role of the managing physician, the model requires close collaboration between the primary care manager and all specialists. The key elements of the PCMH model are shown in Figure 8.7.

FIGURE 8.7

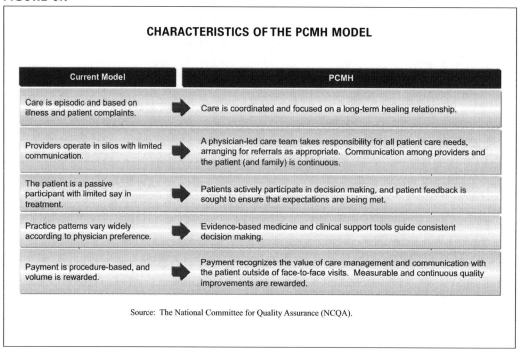

CHARACTERISTICS OF THE PCMH MODEL

Current Model	PCMH
Care is episodic and based on illness and patient complaints.	Care is coordinated and focused on a long-term healing relationship.
Providers operate in silos with limited communication.	A physician-led care team takes responsibility for all patient care needs, arranging for referrals as appropriate. Communication among providers and the patient (and family) is continuous.
The patient is a passive participant with limited say in treatment.	Patients actively participate in decision making, and patient feedback is sought to ensure that expectations are being met.
Practice patterns vary widely according to physician preference.	Evidence-based medicine and clinical support tools guide consistent decision making.
Payment is procedure-based, and volume is rewarded.	Payment recognizes the value of care management and communication with the patient outside of face-to-face visits. Measurable and continuous quality improvements are rewarded.

Source: The National Committee for Quality Assurance (NCQA).

ACOs

An ACO is a new care delivery model that aims to reward clinical integration and care coordination among multiple providers. ACO specifications as defined by payers and providers are evolving, but in general, ACOs can be defined as a local entity and a related set of providers that can be held accountable for the cost and quality of care delivered to a patient population. ACOs require a high degree of financial and clinical integration and are designed to encourage providers to think of themselves as a group with a defined patient population, care delivery goals, and performance metrics. Many hospitals and health systems have identified ACO designation as a significant part of their future vision and

 Strategies for Superior Cardiovascular Service Line Performance

strategic direction. Becoming an ACO will require organizations to shift their focus from care delivery to care management, and it will entail taking on greater financial risk. Despite a lack of clarity regarding the ACO pilot program for Medicare, legislative details suggest ACOs will need to meet the following criteria:

- Agree to become accountable for the overall care for a designated set of Medicare beneficiaries

- Agree to a minimum three-year participation period

- Establish formal management and legal structures that would allow the ACO to provide health services efficiently across the continuum of care

- Include both primary care providers, specialists, and others, to be determined by the Secretary of HHS

- Define processes to promote evidence-based medicine, report on quality and cost measures, and coordinate care

- Demonstrate that it meets patient-centered criteria as determined by the HHS

Lessons Learned

Change has become the norm in cardiac reimbursement for both hospitals and physicians, and these changes will likely continue. Hospitals have experienced a movement to case rates and other bundled payment methodologies, and have increasingly seen CMS focus on exploring new methodologies that emphasize value-based payments. Physicians have seen steady declines in reimbursement, particularly from ancillary services. These changes in reimbursement have had far greater ramifications than simply decreasing the dollars generated from clinical services; they have begun to fundamentally impact modes of care delivery and have changed the complexity of hospital/physician relations.

References

1. "Early Results for FY08 Show Variations in Reimbursement Among Medical Services," *www.ahd. com*, January 5, 2009.

2. Barbara O. Wynn and Molly Scott, "Evaluation of Severity-Adjusted DRG Systems," RAND Health, July 2007.

3. Kevin J. Hayes, Julian Pettengill, and Jeffrey Stensland, "Getting the Price Right: Medicare Payment Rates for Cardiovascular Services," *Health Affairs*, Vol. 26, No. 1, 2007.

4. Ibid.

5. "Hospital Reimbursement: FY2009 Updates to Inpatient Reimbursement Under Medicare," St. Jude Medical, Healthcare Economics, U.S. Division, January 2009.

6. Ibid.

7. CMS-1390 Final Rule FY 2009 IPPS.

8. Ibid.

9. *Dow Jones Newswires*, April 20, 2010.

10. CMS Medicare Fact Sheet, April 19, 2010, *www.cms.gov/acuteinpatientpps/downloads/FSQ09_ IPLTCH11_NPRM041910.pdf*.

11. Originally mandated by Section 501(b) of the Medicare Prescription Drug Improvement and Modernization Act of 2003.

12. CMS Medicare Fact Sheet, April 19, 2010, *www.cms.gov/acuteinpatientpps/downloads/FSQ09_ IPLTCH11_NPRM041910.pdf*.

13. "Outpatient Imaging Forecast: More Volume, Slower Growth, Heightened Competition," *Radiology Business Journal*, March 15, 2008.

14. "Reduced Medicare reimbursement will close nonhospital outpatient cath labs, group warns," *heartwire*, June 10, 2008.

15. Ibid.

16. *www.cms.gov,* July 19, 2010.

17. *www.cms.gov/PhysicianFeeSched/01_Overview.asp#TopOfPage,* July 19, 2010.

CHAPTER 9

Creating a Strategic Advantage With Information Technology

Cardiology is one of the most difficult environments to manage and combine information. There are many best-of-breed vendors that historically have focused on a subset of modality images and exams. So, to get a complete look at a patient's cardiac health, the provider may need to refer to information from several different systems. In addition to modality-specific modules, there are also systems that are designed for a particular function, such as image management or reporting. There is a growing market for integrated multi-modality and multifunction solutions, and many of these systems are created through the merger or acquisition of previously competing vendors.

Some functional requirements of cardiology information systems are common to both the acute care and physician practice settings. The diagram in Figure 9.1 represents a consistent process of cardiac patient care that relies on information systems to enable each step.

FIGURE 9.1

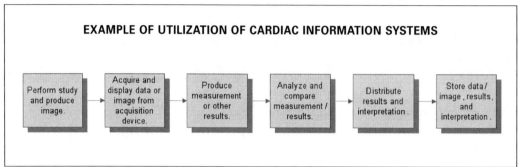

EXAMPLE OF UTILIZATION OF CARDIAC INFORMATION SYSTEMS

Other important system features or options include:

- **Access:** Providers need to be able to review a patient's comprehensive record from a variety of settings, such as the cardiology department, emergency room, operating room, recovery suites, inpatient stay floors, and outpatient office. The option to access information remotely instead of requiring the use of a cardiac read station is an emerging one.

- **Scheduling:** Creating an appointment for a cardiac visit or procedure is not always as simple as scheduling an encounter for a primary care physician. A patient's appointment may need to be done in conjunction with other services in the clinic or hospital, so other resources, rooms, or equipment may need to be scheduled along with the provider visit. In addition, the appointment may need to be in sequence with other events, such as screening laboratory tests and subsequent follow-up care.

- **Work flow:** Systems can be configured to facilitate and coordinate each step of a cardiac procedure. This ensures that the necessary people and

 Strategies for Superior Cardiovascular Service Line Performance

equipment are available and present at the appropriate time and that nothing is overlooked. Ultimately, the clinical staff and the facility may be better utilized and the patient flow may be improved if the work flow elements of information systems are incorporated.

- **Measurement:** Complex algorithms exist in cardiac-specific technology to eliminate human intervention and the related potential for error. As studies are performed, the raw data is converted to industry-standard measurements that can be further analyzed and interpreted.

- **Trending and comparison:** One of the most valuable tools an information system can include is the ability to group like data and present it so that changes over time can be easily detected. Multiple data types can also be trended simultaneously to identify cause-and-effect relationships (e.g., an increase in a medication dose resulting in a decrease in laboratory value).

- **Charge capture and billing:** The revenue cycle component of cardiac care should not be overlooked. Although hospital billing and practice management systems are not necessarily developed specific to cardiology settings, the clinical systems do assist with capturing and accurately coding for all procedures, equipment and device use/implantation, and professional services.

- **Report generation:** Internal and external reports are critical in the cardiology setting. Systems should be able to compile data and create output that includes consultative letters and results, management reports that show performance as it relates to quality indicators, and discrete outcome data, which may be exported to other institutions for research or benchmarking. Entities that require and accept reported process and outcome data for broader analysis and benchmarking include:

- The Society of Thoracic Surgeons
- American College of Cardiology Foundation National Cardiovascular Data Registry
- American Society of Echocardiography
- Society of Cardiovascular Computed Tomography

- **Clinical decision support:** Systems must be able to collect and integrate data to enable informed decision-making on behalf of the clinical care team. This functionality includes interpreting information from a patient's record, such as age, medication history, and pertinent results, and alerting the provider to abnormalities and recommended prophylaxis or interventions according to evidence-based protocols.

- **Outcomes management:** Providers and care teams need to understand current performance to establish and measure progress toward quality improvement goals. Tracking best practice care, such as anticoagulant treatment for patients with chronic atrial fibrillation and routine lipid profiles for coronary artery disease patients, as well as incidence rates for CV events in these patient populations, can help inform improved care.

- **Integration and information exchange:** For the features and functions described here to work optimally, information should be sent to and received from a variety of different entities and systems (see Figure 9.2).

FIGURE 9.2

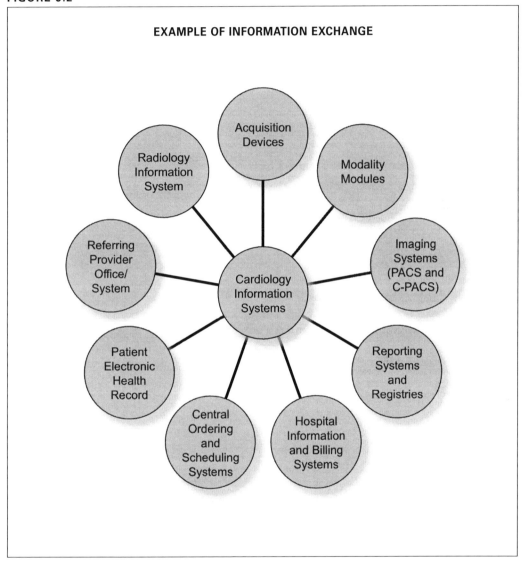

EXAMPLE OF INFORMATION EXCHANGE

Cardiology Hospital Departments

The keys to information system use and value in the acute care setting revolve around information capture and reporting across modalities, many of which may have unique systems that capture the image or exam output. The following are examples of some of the ancillary testing modalities that need to be captured:

- Cardiopulmonary exercise testing

- Echocardiography

- Electrocardiography

- Nuclear cardiography

- Cardiac catheterizations

- Hemodynamics monitoring

- Stress exams

- Computed tomography (CT) angiography

- Cardiac magnetic resonance

- Holter and event monitoring

- Vascular ultrasound

System types

The types of systems used throughout the process of capturing and reporting patient data include the following.

  Strategies for Superior Cardiovascular Service Line Performance

Acquisition devices

Diagnostic cardiology products capture information collected directly from the patient. These devices can produce direct output in the form of a printed report, or they can connect and upload results to other systems to create a more comprehensive record. Other features include downloading demographics and orders, distributing reports via e-mail or fax, storing results for future review, and generating billing information for automated or manual charge capture. Some of the most common devices are used for electrocardiograms (EKG), cardiac stress (treadmill) tests, and Holter monitor analysis.

Modality-specific information systems

Modality modules automate the processing and storage of individual exams and procedures. They allow care teams to display, analyze and interpret, print, and archive results. The analysis and interpretation involves performing serial comparisons of previously completed studies without having to rely on manual review of multiple printouts stored in a paper medical record. Most modality information systems are compatible with multiple acquisition device vendors so that, for instance, EKG tracings collected and interfaced from several different products can be easily compared. Modality modules can integrate with a more holistic CV information system (CVIS) so that exams can be stored in a patient's record alongside other modality images and reports. These systems, such as EKG management and hemodynamics monitoring systems, commonly incorporate work flow management tools specific to the exam type.

CVISs

A CVIS performs CV study digital image and information management. The primary benefits of using a CVIS are its abilities to provide a central repository for all cardiac-related data and to streamline and simplify the related work flows and subsequent reporting. It can be deployed in one of two ways, or in a hybrid fashion. The first option for deployment, and the more common, is to collect images and information from a variety of different sources (including the "best of breed" systems. The second option is for the CVIS to include modules for all of the different modalities so that an integrated database is available, avoiding expensive and sometimes troublesome interfaces. Although CVISs are becoming more robust, especially as demand for them continues to increase, most experts agree that a completely unified and stand-alone solution that meets the needs of all modalities is still a work in progress. There is growing penetration of these systems, especially in academic teaching institutions and large urban hospitals. Many acquisition scenarios are first-time versus replacement purchases, indicating an emerging market.

Cardiology Picture Archiving and Communication Systems

Picture Archiving and Communication System (PACS) medical imaging solutions, which emerged, at least in concept, in the early 1980s, are used to provide on-site and remote access to images; to store images digitally so that they can be integrated with other systems, such as hospital information systems and electronic health records (EHR); and, more recently, to manage the work flow of performing and interpreting exams. PACS have significant penetration for use with x-rays, ultrasounds, magnetic resonance images, and mammograms.

Cardiology PACS (C-PACS) is not as widespread as radiology PACS, but it is gaining momentum, especially in catheterization and echocardiography laboratories. The implementation of radiology PACS results in a significant savings for an organization, as it involves the replacement of film generation and storage. Cardiology images are usually already stored in a digital format, so the economic advantage of introducing a C-PACS is much less compelling. These solutions are beginning to include options for CT, intravascular ultrasound, and nuclear cardiology, and they are anticipated to become more common.

Inventory management systems

Inventory management systems have been a critical part of hospital operations for many years. However, as equipment—cardiac especially—has become more costly and difficult to track because of new product releases, expiration dates, and recalls, organizations are looking for sophisticated options that require less manual processing. As a result, systems have emerged that are built specifically to manage the inventory of cardiology medical items, particularly in interventional suites. Common features of these systems include the use of:

- Radio frequency identification (RFID) so that items can be uniquely tagged and scanned

- Storage units that automatically read all of the RFID tags at a defined interval to produce an almost real-time inventory by tracking items as they are added, removed, and replaced

- RFID scanning equipment in the location of use or implantation so that both distribution and use of items is recorded

As a result of systems like these, hospitals can give physicians a wider variety of product options without having to carry an unnecessarily large inventory. Both the waste associated with unused products prior to their expiration as well as instances of product unavailability are reduced. Charge capture is also improved. From the perspective of patient safety, some solutions include the option to activate alerts if providers or other clinical staff are planning to use a product that has expired or been recalled.

System vendors

Companies that have presence in the acute care CVIS and C-PACS market space are listed in Figure 9.3.

FIGURE 9.3

CARDIOLOGY SYSTEM VENDORS

Agfa	Digisonics	Epic Systems Corporation
FUJIFILM Medical Systems USA, Inc.	GE Healthcare	Goodroe Healthcare Solutions
Heart Imaging Technologies, LLC	LUMEDX Corporation	McKesson Corp.
Merge Healthcare	Philips	ScImage
Siemens Healthcare	Solution 64	Thinking Systems Corporation

Cardiology Physician Practices

Cardiology physician practices have many of the same system needs as hospital departments, and in many cases they use similar, if not the same, systems as those described in the previous section. Practices, however, are often tasked with longer-term and less episodic patient care, and as such, a more complete and longitudinal EHR is appropriate. This record will include additional tracking features, such as sophisticated health maintenance and disease management functionality, that involve the patient in their ongoing care. The documentation requirements in the practice setting go beyond studies and exams and include routine physician office visits and monitoring done by other clinic staff, such as nurses and case managers. A physician practice can use EHR systems that are available for use by all primary and specialty care practices, leveraging existing cardiology-specific modifications and/or creating new ones, or it can select a cardiology-specific product option, although there are relatively few available in the market.

EHR cardiology features and functions

There are unique requirements that a practice must consider when selecting, implementing, or optimizing its EHR solution.

- **Documentation tools:** Templates or other documentation tools should exist that facilitate CV-related data capture of relevant information, such as cardiac history, cardiac risk factors, and cardiac procedure, as well as study documentation, including discrete measurements.

- **Device interfacing:** In comparison to cardiology practices, primary care and most other specialty practice settings do not require the same degree of disparate system data sharing. Work flows and data access will be improved if the EHR can receive information and vital signs from EKG machines and implantable devices.

- **Evidence-based protocols and algorithms:** The EHR can help enable informed decision-making by automatically identifying results and measurements in the patient's record that deviate from normal ranges. The system also may be able to combine and evaluate multiple data types to alert the healthcare team to appropriate prophylaxis or intervention. For example, an analysis of EKG interpretations, ejection fraction (EF) measurements, medication and problem lists, laboratory results, and CV history elements may indicate that the patient should be started on angiotensin-converting enzyme (ACE) inhibitor or angiotensin receptor blocker (ARB) therapy. The alert may include documented evidence and references and also require that the provider document exceptions or inaction to the alert.

- **Reports:** Consultative letters and procedural reports are needed for referring providers. The cardiology practice may create "canned" options that individual physicians can modify, as needed, so that they are complete but understandable.

- **Implantable device monitoring:** The EHR can potentially be interfaced with implantable device vendors and the actual devices themselves. Patient enrollment information from vendors monitoring remote defibrillators and pacemakers can be imported so that the practice also does appropriate monitoring for its patient population. Information can be transmitted directly from the implanted devices so that the care team can be made aware of device abnormalities, patient arrhythmias, etc. If transmitted to the EHR, irregularities can be analyzed and interpreted in the context of the complete medical record. This integration can also allow the practice to quickly identify and notify patients if their implanted device is recalled.

- **Anticoagulation monitoring:** Unique documentation tools and encounter forms may be used to treat patients being managed on anticoagulation therapy. It is critical that drug and laboratory values be captured discretely to allow for comparison and trending. The care team can also produce reports to identify patients who are overdue for their laboratory tests so that appropriate outreach can be performed.

- **Access to healthcare resources:** The EHR may either be embedded with or provide online access to tools such as risk factor calculators, registries or reporting institutions, and studies from other organizations.

The Certification Commission for Healthcare Information Technology

The Certification Commission for Healthcare Information Technology (CCHIT) is the organization that certifies EHRs as recognized by the U.S. Department of Health & Human Services. It expanded its process in 2007 and 2008 to launch two additional certification options for ambulatory EHR solutions: CV medicine and CV medicine with advanced reporting. At the time of this publication, there are 11 vendors certified in CV medicine, two of which have the advanced reporting designation (see Figure 9.4).

FIGURE 9.4

VENDORS WITH CCHIT CERTIFICATION

Vendor	CV Medicine (2008 Certification)	CV Medicine With Advanced Reporting (2011 Certification)
AdvancedMD Software, Inc.	X	
e-MDs	X	
Gateway Electronic Medical Management Systems	X	
GE Healthcare	X	
gloStream, Inc.	X	
Greenway Medical Technologies, Inc.	X	X
MedInformatix Inc.	X	
NextGen Healthcare Information Systems, Inc.	X	X
Sage	X	
Secure Infosys, LLC	X	
STI Computer Services, Inc.	X	

Source: Certification Commission for Health Information Technology, June 2010

The 2011 CV medicine certification will require system functionality that supports the 28 identified criteria, described in Figure 9.5.

   Strategies for Superior Cardiovascular Service Line Performance

FIGURE 9.5

CRITERIA FOR 2011 CV MEDICINE CERTIFICATION

Category	Criteria
Data Retention, Availability, and Searchability	The system shall provide the ability to import (and/or directly enter) the final report of studies/procedures from systems external to the EHR. The system shall provide the ability to search for a particular study/procedure for a given patient based on date or name of study/procedure.
Data Retrieval	The system shall provide access to view, through the user interface (UI) of the EHR, the final report of studies/procedures imported from external sources (and/or directly entered into the EHR).
Data Output	The system shall provide the ability to export the final report of studies/procedures stored in the EHR.
Key Discrete Data Elements	The system shall provide the ability to capture the following data elements for EF as discrete data: (1) date of test, (2) modality of test, (3) quantitative value as a percentage, and (4) qualitative value (narrative). The system shall provide the ability to store the following data elements for a stress test as discrete data: (1) date of study; (2) test type—list to include at least: exercise treadmill, exercise echo, dobutamine echo, exercise nuclear, adenosine nuclear, dobutamine nuclear, dipyridamole nuclear, adenosine MRI, dobutamine MRI, adenosine PET/CT, and dipyridamole PET/CT; (3) CPT coded test type; (4) and result (normal, abnormal, indeterminate). The system shall provide the ability to store the following data elements for invasive electrophysiology procedures as discrete data: (1) date of procedure, (2) CPT coded test type (multiple selection capability required), (3) procedure(s) performed (selected from customizable list of options; multiple selection capability required), and (4) ID of physician(s) performing procedure (multiple input capability required).

FIGURE 9.5

CRITERIA FOR 2011 CV MEDICINE CERTIFICATION (CONT.)

Category	Criteria
Key Discrete Data Elements (Continued from previous page)	The system shall provide the ability to store the following data elements for cardiac catheterization as discrete data: (1) date of procedure, (2) CPT coded test type (multiple selection capability required), (3) procedure name, (4) type of intervention(s) (selected from customizable list of options; multiple selection capability required), and (5) ID of physician(s) performing procedure (multiple input capability required). The system shall provide the ability to store the following data elements for cardiothoracic surgeries as discrete data elements: (1) date of procedure, (2) CPT coded test type (multiple selection capability required), (3) procedure(s) performed (selected from customizable list of options; multiple selection capability required), and (4) ID of physician(s) performing procedure (multiple input capability required). The system shall provide the ability to store the following implant/device data elements as discrete data: (1) date of implant/procedure, (2) type of device, (3) product name, (4) device manufacturer (selected from customizable list of options), (5) product specifications (e.g., diameter, length), (6) product serial number, (7) manufacturer model number, (8) leads type (for pacemaker), (9) date removed, and (10) physical location of device implant. The system shall be capable of documenting current and past tobacco use in a quantitative fashion. The system shall be capable of documenting that tobacco cessation counseling was provided, including a date stamp. The system shall provide the ability to store the following data elements for EKG as discrete data: (1) date and time of procedure, (2) date ordered, and (3) EKG interpretation.

FIGURE 9.5

CRITERIA FOR 2011 CV MEDICINE CERTIFICATION (CONT.)	
Category	**Criteria**
EF	The system shall provide the ability to retrieve and display EF results from multiple studies/procedures/modalities in one view (simultaneously), inclusive of EF (quantitative or qualitative) date and modality. The system shall provide the ability to graphically display EF results from multiple studies/procedures/modalities in one view (simultaneously).
Data Associations	The system shall provide the ability to link data regarding a device implanted to the implantation procedure and display both sets of data in surgical summaries and reports. The system shall provide the ability to link procedure data with patient diagnosis.
Problem List	The system shall provide the ability to configure the sorting/view of the problem list at the level of the specialty.
Laboratory Results	The system shall provide the ability to document, in structured fields, a target range, a target maximum, or a target minimum for lab results customized to the patient for the following lab values: (1) international normalized ratio (INR), (2) total cholesterol, (3) low-density lipoprotein (LDL), (4) high-density lipoprotein (HDL), (5) Triglycerides, and (6) HbA1c. The system shall provide the ability to indicate when the patient is outside their custom target for the following lab values: (1) INR, (2) total cholesterol, (3) LDL, (4) HDL, (5) Triglycerides, and (6) HbA1c.
History and Risk Factors	The system shall provide the ability to create a CV-specific risk factor panel/display. This should include, but is not limited to, the following: diabetes, hyperlipidemia, hypertension, history of CV disease, family history, and tobacco use. The system shall provide the ability to create a CV-specific family history panel/display. This should include, but is not limited to, the following: coronary disease and sudden death.

FIGURE 9.5

CRITERIA FOR 2011 CV MEDICINE CERTIFICATION (CONT.)	
Category	**Criteria**
Vital Signs	The system shall provide the ability to document and display vital sign measurements collected outside of the current patient encounter. The system shall provide the ability to include vital sign measurements collected outside a patient encounter in trend worksheets.
UI	The system shall provide the ability to display a summary screen (or screens) of CV-relevant patient information when a patient record is viewed. The following constitutes a minimum list of the types of patient information that shall be available through the summary view: (1) problem list, (2) medications, (3) allergies, (4) labs, (5) CV tests and procedures (diagnostic), (6) CV tests and procedures (therapeutic), and (7) implants/devices.
Report Viewing	The system shall provide the ability to display the accurate (i.e., non-distorted) tracing from any EKG stored in the system or imported from another system.
Access	The system will allow secure remote access to patient data. The system will provide the ability to emergently transmit specific patient data, reports, and accurate, clinically interpretable images to alternate providers/facilities.

Cardiology Resources and Initiatives

There are several national and international initiatives and organizations that support efforts to improve cardiology care and outcomes by leveraging information technology. Two examples are described in more detail next.

Integrating the Healthcare Enterprise

Integrating the Healthcare Enterprise is an initiative supported by technology and healthcare institutions that was created to encourage and enable information exchange so that a patient's medical record is as complete as possible.[1] In 2004, an effort specific to the integration of information within cardiology began. Participants include the American College of Cardiology, the American Society of Echocardiography, the American Society of Nuclear Cardiology, the Society for Cardiovascular Angiography and Interventions, and the European Society of Cardiology. The following eight cardiology integration profiles, with technical frameworks and specifications, have been designed to help organizations make better decisions and achieve clinical goals through better use of data:

- Cardiac catheterization and work flow

- Echocardiography work flow

- Implantable device cardiac observation

- Retrieve EKG for display

- Displayable reports

- Evidence documents

- Nuclear medical imaging

- Stress testing work flow integration

Bridges to Excellence

Bridges to Excellence (BTE) is a coalition developed by employers, physicians, and healthcare industry experts to incent and reward quality patient care.[2] Focused initially on diabetes and CV disease, BTE recognizes the role and importance of information technology and, in addition to incorporating rewards related to the adoption of effective systems, relies on data that can be produced and provided only if sophisticated technology is in place. The BTE program includes four "care links" related to cardiac care, as detailed in Figure 9.6.

Strategies for Superior Cardiovascular Service Line Performance

FIGURE 9.6

BTE CARE LINKS

BTE Care Link	Measures
Cardiac	Blood pressure (BP) control LDL control Complete lipid profile Use of aspirin or another antithrombotic Smoking status and cessation advice and treatment
Congestive Heart Failure	Beta blocker therapy ACE-Inhibitor/ARB therapy Left ventricular failure assessment Weight measurement Assessment of clinical symptoms of volume overload Assessment of activity level Patient education
Coronary Artery Disease	BP control LDL control Evaluation of activity level and anginal symptoms Smoking status and cessation advice and treatment Complete lipid profile LDL drug therapy Use of aspirin or other antiplatelet therapy ACE-Inhibitor/ARB therapy Betablocker treatment after a heart attack Continued betablocker therapy
Hypertension	BP control LDL control Complete lipid profile Use of aspirin or another antithrombotic Urine protein test Annual serum creatinine test Smoking status and cessation advice and treatment Diabetes mellitus documentation or screening test Documentation of counseling for diet and physical activity

Lessons Learned

There is widespread interest in consolidating the cardiac patient record, and pressure on the relevant vendors is anticipated to result in streamlined and simplified cardiology device, information, and image management systems over time. Integration among various vendors and systems, however, continues to be a critical and time-consuming activity among cardiology departments and physician practices. There is growing support in the industry to select and connect the right cardiology systems so that the superior decision-making associated with complete data is not dependent on integrated system advances. Development and use of additional functionality, such as telemedicine tools and patient portals with health risk assessment calculators, is on a parallel path to integration, and ultimately, the patient will be more involved with a healthcare team that has electronic access to a current and comprehensive record.

References

1. For more information, *www.ihe.net.*

2. For more information, *www.bridgestoexcellence.org.*

     Strategies for Superior Cardiovascular Service Line Performance